CW01183531

CAZ MOONEY'S BUDGETING PLANNER

Caz Mooney is a mum of three who runs the successful social-media accounts @Irishbudgeting, where she shares practical advice and tips on how to budget, save money and tackle debt. She lives in County Offaly with her husband and three children.

CAZ MOONEY'S BUDGETING PLANNER

TAKE CONTROL OF YOUR MONEY

AND ACHIEVE YOUR FINANCIAL GOALS

Gill Books

Gill Books
Hume Avenue
Park West
Dublin 12
www.gillbooks.ie

Gill Books is an imprint of M.H. Gill and Co.

© Caz Mooney 2023

978 07171 9754 5

Designed by Typo•glyphix, Burton-on-Trent, DE14 3HE
Proofread by Alicia McAuley
Printed and bound by BZ Graf, Poland
This book is typeset in 12/16 pt Depot New

The paper used in this book comes from the wood pulp of sustainably managed forests.

All rights reserved.
No part of this publication may be copied, reproduced or transmitted in any form or by any means, without written permission of the publishers.

A CIP catalogue record for this book is available from the British Library.

5 4 3 2 1

For anyone who has no money at the end of the month.
Time for a change!

Contents

Part One
Background to budgeting — 1

- Hi, I'm Caz — 2
- Budgeting — 9
- Savings — 28
- Debt — 32
- Making your money stretch — 38

Part Two
The year ahead — 49

- Monthly goals — 49
- Let's get more specific with our goals! — 53
- Where do you want to be five years from now? — 54
- Career goals and future plans — 55
- Your vision board — 56
- Memberships, subscriptions and large expenses — 58
- What's coming up this year? — 60
- Saving your sinking funds — 61
- Savings tracker — 62
- Debts tracker — 64

CONTENTS

Bills and direct debits tracker	66
Income tracker	68
Special occasions and gifts tracker	70

Part Three
How to track your spending — 73

Beginning your budget	74

Part Four
Let's get tracking — 87

Month one	89
Month two	114
Month three	139
Month four	164
Month five	189
Month six	214
Month seven	239
Month eight	264
Month nine	289
Month ten	314
Month eleven	339
Month twelve	364
In case of emergency	389

Acknowledgements	390

Part One

Background to budgeting

Hi, I'm Caz

I'm a mum of three kids who are thirteen, ten and one, and my family is no different from the many other families in Ireland navigating the current financial climate. We started our budgeting journey in 2018, when my husband and I were hit by the realisation that we had to make a change.

That year we had gone on a few holidays, had a lovely big credit-card bill and realised that we would never get the keys for our own home if we didn't change up our financial circumstances. The rental shortage had hit, there were very few places available in our area and we were worried … It was now or never.

Over the next year, we made changes to our finances, overhauled our way of thinking and took control of our money. We had decided to try a 'low-spend' year, and during that period we cleared that credit-card bill and saved over €15,000 towards our house deposit. By October of that year we had the keys for our own home in our hands! Since then, we have become completely debt-free – apart from our mortgage – and continue to use the same principles and habits to change our family's financial future.

I started sharing and documenting my family's journey on social media in mid-December 2021. It started out as an anonymous account. I was on a career break after having my youngest and we were down to a single income. I guess making things public helped with accountability, but I had also been following a few American financial pages and, as we had been on a financial journey ourselves in 2018, I liked the idea of sharing tips to help families like mine. Over time I shared more and started to show my face, and from there it just grew.

Hearing stories of families like mine and followers just like me clearing debt, going on holidays that they saved for and getting the keys for their first homes has been the most rewarding thing. I love to hear your wins – they are such a boost, and they can be a great way of picking yourself up when you are struggling. There's something about hearing about even the smallest win that is just so motivating!

A journey is never all plain sailing. There are twists and turns and little bumps in the road – but knowing that others are taking the same road makes the journey less lonely, and hearing that someone has taken that first step also reminds you of how far you have come.

I share many of my tips and tricks online, but I wanted there to be a place that contained everything you need: the tools and the tips to improve your finances and change your future. This book is going to contain your journey. Some of you may have been tracking your spending already, and some of you may be right at the start of your budgeting journey. Whatever stage you're at, I hope that by the end of this planner, you'll feel more confident about managing your money and be well on your way to changing your financial future.

I know you may be stressed and feeling worried about money. Before we started our journey, we were the same – living paycheque to paycheque, worried about how we were going to afford school uniforms, struggling to afford fuel for the car, burdened by our debt. However, I want you to make a promise to yourself now: that you will start this journey, stay consistent and give it your all for the next few months … I can guarantee that you'll notice an improvement in your finances, and you'll be one step closer to your goals!

How to use this book

It can be overwhelming to try and overhaul a large area of your life, particularly if you're attempting to break habits that you've lived with since you were a child – believe me, I know. To help make things as easy and as clear as possible, I have divided this book into four sections.

- This first section details my own experience: the lessons I learned and the steps my family took to save our deposit, take control of our finances and become debt-free (apart from our mortgage). I'll break the basics of budgeting down into simple steps, making sure that you have the language and tools to get started on your budgeting journey.

- In the second section, you'll be setting your own financial goals, breaking them up into manageable, attainable targets that you can work towards during your financial journey. These goals are going to become a reality, so let's see what you need to do to make them happen!

- In the third section, I'll walk you through setting up your own budget, using tips and examples every step of the way so that you'll soon be ready to do it yourself.

- The fourth and final section is your space to begin budgeting: to properly start working towards your financial goals and changing your financial health. You'll be putting pen to paper and taking control of your own income and expenses. It's time to start the journey!

Money mentality

When you think about money, what are the three words that come to mind?

When I was growing up, friends and family didn't talk about money. It was something that was shameful – taboo, almost. If you were doing well financially, it would be seen as bragging to tell people that; and if you were struggling, you were just to say that you were 'grand' and brush it under the rug. I would see a neighbour driving a nice car and wonder how they had afforded it; I would hear about someone being promoted and assume they were now earning great money.

Imagine if, instead, people were more open about their finances. Maybe that neighbour bought that car on finance, an impulse purchase that they now regret. Perhaps that promotion came with more money but longer working hours, and so a larger childcare cost.

One thing that I found interesting is that the more I started opening up about my family's finances, the more others opened up to me about theirs. I was able to learn from other people's struggles – and be motivated by their success!

I think it is important to release the feelings of guilt and shame that we may have around money. Personally, I feel that the best way to begin doing this is to become familiar with your debt and to no longer brush it under the carpet – the unknown is always scarier. Instead, you are going to communicate with those who are also affected and start working towards paying it off. When you write down your initial debt figures, your starting numbers, take a moment to look at them ... this is the last time that you will see those numbers. It can be emotionally difficult to discover the true amount of debt that you have to pay, but it's such an important step on your journey. You should include your partner, if involved, as talking about finances and sharing this information will help you both to be on the same page. I'll talk more about the involvement of partners and family later.

You are moving from a fixed mindset and towards a growth mindset. With a fixed mindset, you may struggle with change or struggle to look at your situation from a different point of view. A growth mindset, however, is one in which you are ready to learn and to adapt. Your financial situation has already happened; it is how you deal with that situation that matters. This is no small change to make, and it can be hard to shake off your shame, guilt and stress, but as you continue along this journey, month by month, it will get easier and easier. It's time to change the way you think about money: your money is no longer going to control you, you're going to control it!

The big picture

The three main areas that we're going to look at are **savings**, **debt** and **budgeting**.

You are going to start your savings journey immediately. The first goal that I recommend you work towards is your emergency fund. I know you will have other goals that you want to get started on, perhaps more exciting ones – but a sudden, unexpected cost could really set back your overall progress, so this will be your safety net in case of that.

Next up, let's look at any debt that you have. If you are starting your budgeting journey with debt, you're far from the only one! We started off this way ourselves and clearing our debt has been a massive part of our journey so far. It's the step I would advise that you try to take as soon as you have saved your emergency fund; there's little point in building up further savings if you're paying interest on a mountain of debt. In the long run, it's better to prioritise this at the start, even if you feel like you're just sending your money straight back out the door. But imagine what you'll be able to do with your money once you aren't putting it towards debt. Imagine the peace of mind that freedom from debt will bring!

Both debt and savings are linked by budgeting; learning to budget your income is the tool that will help you to save and to clear your debt. If debt and savings are things that you can have, budgeting is your course of action, the plan where you give your money a job. It's the key to turning around your financial situation. I'm going to show you how to break this plan down into manageable steps so that you can budget with confidence and gain financial peace of mind.

Structuring your goals

It can be hard to know when to start when you set out to overhaul your finances. How do you know which goals to work towards first? How do you know where to send your extra income?

First things first: you'll need to **learn how to budget**. We'll be talking about this later in the book in much more practical depth, but this is a crucial step, as it gives you the necessary information about what money you can put towards your financial goals. Your budget will be the plan, the roadmap to helping you work on your other goals.

Of these, your first goal absolutely must be to **save your emergency fund**. This is vital, as it's unfortunately an inevitable fact of life that something will crop up – an expense that you didn't plan for, something that would knock your progress. Again, I'll return to this later on, but about €1,000 would suit most budgets as a solid emergency fund. You can always increase this fund once you've paid off your debt, with many people choosing to save enough to cover a few months' expenses – not your income, but the bare bones.

Your next goal should be to **clear your debt**. (You might be tempted to head straight for this step and skip saving your emergency fund – but your progress will all be for nothing if you don't protect your budget in case of emergencies.)

That total number may seem overwhelming to start with, but there are different ways of tackling your debt, and we can find the method that works for you. Plus, once you start this habit, you'll never have to see that overwhelming number again!

After becoming debt-free, or if you had no debt to begin with, your next step is to look at what other **things you would like to save towards**. Some great examples might be a house deposit, a wedding, house renovations, a new car ... or, of course, expanding that faithful emergency fund.

What happens if you have to use your emergency fund, or at least part of it? Well, then you must pause your debt pay-off or saving and go back to the first step. You must save that emergency fund back up before you continue. And what about saving for birthdays, Christmas, a holiday next year and other future expenses? These expenses that you can plan for are called sinking funds, and you will save towards them from the beginning. It's important to reduce the financial stress that these often-large expenses will have on your budget by setting aside a little each month towards them.

Staying motivated

Setting financial goals is so important in terms of motivation. Without knowing what you are working towards, in detail, it will be so much more difficult to keep going. These goals must be important to you, otherwise the potential reward won't stop you from being tempted to overspend. I suggest breaking your long-term goals into manageable chunks – monthly goals also. It is such a great feeling at the end of the month to be able to tick off those goals!

Tell friends and family what you're doing. Try to set aside any feelings of awkwardness around discussing money or cutting back. We are living through a cost-of-living crisis – if ever there was a time for it to be entirely understandable for someone to want to get a handle on their finances, this is it! And having friends and family to cheer you on will really help to keep you accountable.

It's also helpful to think about where you want to be in the future. We'll talk more about this later in the book, but it is important to look further down the line than just the year ahead. Our primary motivation, for example, was to get the keys to our own home. I visualised those keys in my hand, and the day they were handed to me was the most surreal moment.

Even within a strict budget, be sure to make room for the things that are important to you. Set aside some money for you to spend on yourself! And the same goes for everyone else in your house. If your budget is too strict, you are unlikely to stick to it. It's just like dieting: when your diet is too restrictive, you won't be able to keep it up. If it is important to you to go for coffee with friends every week, then do that. Or if you like to have a takeaway every Friday evening for family movie night, go for it! Yes, you would probably reach your financial goals more quickly if you put all of your income beyond essentials towards those goals ... but you would struggle to stick to such a strict budget for any length of time. I would rather that your budget was manageable, and that you were still able to enjoy the things that are important to your family and yourself.

Above all, take a moment to celebrate your wins. The size of your celebration may depend on the goal, and the length of time it took to reach it, but it is important to acknowledge every single win along your journey – because each win brings you closer to the biggest win. Some of our celebrations in the past have included getting a takeaway with family, going to kids' club in the cinema or even driving to the beach (quite a novelty, given that we live in the midlands!). So treat yourself to acknowledge all that you've already achieved – and then pause for just a second and think about how proud you'll be when you and your family reach that ultimate goal!

Budgeting

Now that we've covered the basics of a financial strategy, it's time to go into a little more detail. There are several different methods of budgeting, and each one has its advantages and disadvantages. Here are some of the more popular methods of budgeting.

Pay-yourself-first, or reverse budget

This is a simple budgeting method where the first thing you do when you get paid each month is to send a certain amount towards the debt and savings goals that you have. This amount is usually a significant portion of your wages, and you must then make do with what is left over.

Payday ⇨ savings/debt ⇨ needs/fixed expenses ⇨ wants/variable expenses

This is a great method for someone who has fewer expenses, or who struggles to keep on top of their finances. However, it does mean that you often aren't changing your spending habits. This is because you are not creating a plan for every cent, and so you may be putting less towards your goals than you could do. Another budgeting method may allow you to save more money, pay off more debt and reach your financial goals faster.

50/30/20 budget

This is where you break down your income into three categories of expenses:

1. 50 per cent towards necessary and fixed expenses
2. 30 per cent towards variable spending
3. 20 per cent towards your financial goals (savings and debt)

This method is great for people who like to automate their budget. It's particularly handy if you're on a fixed income; you can have those amounts sent to different accounts automatically each payday. However, for many, income varies, and expenses can also vary from month to month. I personally felt that this method didn't work for our family, as some months we simply didn't have 20 **per cent** left after expenses, while other months we had more money and so wanted to throw more than 20 **per cent** towards our debt.

Incremental budgeting

This is when you look at your expenses for the previous year and then increase or decrease a percentage, depending on your lifestyle, wages and expenses for the current year. You can then divide this total into a monthly projected budget, or even a weekly budget. This is a more complicated means of budgeting than the previous two methods, and it does tend to be more associated with businesses. It's perhaps more suited to a personal budget when that person has been budgeting for a while.

Zero-based budgeting

I use a method called zero-based budgeting when writing my budget. This is where you budget every single euro of your income. Leaving a certain amount of money in your account that has no job might feel comforting when you first start budgeting, but in my experience, it is just too tempting to spend it!

Instead, by budgeting every euro of your paycheque, you are giving your money a job. This puts you in control of your money. You decide where it's spent – how much goes towards each category or goal – and all before that money even enters your account.

This method was a game-changer for my family's budget. Instead of having vague intentions with our income, we were deliberate in how we allocated it, and that makes a big difference when you are working on goals. If every euro is budgeted for, and if, after bills, food and other necessary categories, you are committed to putting the rest of your income towards your next financial goal … then you're going to reach that goal so much sooner.

One of the concerns that some people have with this method is a fear of not having extra money in their account for unexpected events. *This is why we have our emergency fund.* I know that with the first paycheque you use to plan and implement your first budget, it will feel very strange to allocate every euro. It will feel especially strange if you plan to cash budget — to withdraw everything except the money for bills — but have faith: this method works and works well. It's such an amazing feeling to know that you are back in control of your finances, creating a plan for your income instead of letting your income decide how you live your life.

Cash budgeting

It regularly surprises people when I mention that I cash budget all of my everyday expenses. The idea that, in this day and age, someone is paying in cash instead of tapping their card or their smartphone is often baffling.

When I started cash budgeting, or cash stuffing, I wasn't sure that it would be for me either ... but I was desperate to give it a try. I was struggling with overspending every time I went to the shop. It was just too easy to tap the card and have no idea if I had left enough for bread and milk the next week.

So, I decided to give cash budgeting a go. I told myself what I will tell you: give it three months. I know that seems like a long time, but it can take a little while to get into the swing of things, as with all budgeting. It was only when I noticed that, come payday, I wasn't checking my account, waiting for the money to go in, that I realised that it was working for me. I actually even forgot it was payday!

I feel like it's just so much harder to overspend cash. It's physical, and its value seems so much more tangible — €50 in your hand versus one tap of your card. Cash can also be divided up easily, allowing you to budget it physically. I divide mine in a binder, but paper envelopes also work well in the beginning.

STARTING CASH STUFFING

I cash budget almost everything in my total budget, the only exceptions being sinking funds, bills and occasional online purchases. Everything else, all the variables, I budget for with cash: food, diesel, personal spending, etc. However, you can start by taking out cash for just one or two envelopes, and using them for the areas that you overspend in. Some of the more popular cash-envelope categories are:

- Groceries
- Petrol or diesel
- Household expenses
- Eating out
- Clothing
- Beauty
- Kids' activities
- Pocket money
- Pets
- Charity
- Miscellaneous

The number of categories for which you wish to cash budget will depend on your family, but I would start out with only a few, to avoid becoming overwhelmed, and then add categories as you need them.

For myself, I started by getting some colourful paper envelopes from a stationery shop and writing my different categories on the front of the envelopes. Once I knew that this method was working well for our family's budget and I was used to the routine – of planning, taking out my cash, dividing it between the envelopes and using them as needed – I then invested in a cash binder.

A cash binder is a small A5 binder with pockets for your cash. Nowadays you can get these from lots of online stores: just search the words 'cash binder'. Many Irish small businesses are now also selling personalised binders online, which is where mine is from, and with that you get the added benefit of supporting another local business. The envelopes can be cardboard or plastic zipped pockets, and they will feel a little more secure than your paper envelopes.

When you have completed your budget, on payday simply take out the total amount of cash and divide it up into your envelopes. If you need smaller notes, taking your cash out of the post office or credit union will allow you to request your withdrawal in certain denominations (and certain banks will do this too).

I don't carry all my cash envelopes around with me; instead, I decide how much I want to spend before leaving the house, take that amount out of the relevant envelope(s) and pop it into my purse. You can get very fancy purses nowadays that have pockets for all your different categories, but I simply laminated dividers for my purse and labelled them. Deciding ahead of time how much you want to spend takes a little getting used to, but it has helped me stick to my budget and reduce impulse spending so much. If it's not there, you can't spend it!

Looking after the pennies

A question I regularly get asked is: what to do with the coins? Personally, I use the coins up first when buying something. Say I am buying a few messages from my local shop and the total comes to €12.50. I use €2.50 in coins, and then I'm only looking for a €10 note. Some people also save their coins, and you could use that saved change for something fun or put it towards one of your financial goals.

By using cash, it's so much easier to stick to your budget for each category. Need to do a food shop? The money is there in the envelope. You don't have to worry about overspending; the total amount that you have budgeted towards that category is there, and once it's gone, it's gone.

What if I have cash left over in my envelopes?

That's up to you – it's always a thrill to decide what to do with this extra cash! You can decide to take that money out and put it towards your goals or you can let it build up. I find that it often depends on the category. For example, if it's my diesel envelope, I will often let it build up, as this category goes up and down for me, depending on the amount of driving I do. If you decide to remove the cash from the envelope, you should add this amount of extra income to your next budget to keep a note of it, and then put it towards the goal you are working on. If you are budgeting correctly, however, having leftover cash like this shouldn't be something that happens regularly. You'll become a pro at budgeting and know exactly how much you need in each category.

What if cash budgeting isn't for me?

No problem — I have a similar method that works well for many. In fact, it's how my husband budgets and it's been really helpful for him ... online saving pots! These are like virtual envelopes; you can even name them and divide your money into the different categories. This gives you the control of cash envelopes, while also allowing you to spend online and not have to worry about having change.

There are many providers of this service, including banks — both digital and high street — post-office accounts and even some credit unions. As with cash budgeting, there are pros and cons to this method, and it may not be for everybody. I use these online pots to save my sinking funds, but it wouldn't work as well for helping me to avoid impulse spending. The tap-tap aspect of a card is still there and I feel it would be much easier to justify overspending, as well as to move the money around the envelopes. It also can take a day or two for money to transfer back to your bank account, so I would still recommend leaving enough in your main account to cover bills.

These pots are a great method if you want to start budgeting and aren't ready to commit to cash stuffing, and they also take less time, as you don't need to go get the cash out. As I've said, many people will find that a mixture of both methods works well for them. They may only cash-budget areas that they tend to overspend in, and use saving pots for the rest.

Everyday expenses

Your everyday expenses are the expenses that your family spends daily and/or monthly on variable costs, meaning that the total may go up or down. These costs can often be somewhat reduced, when necessary, or they can increase. As you get to know your budget, you'll learn what works for your finances, and many of these categories will be a similar amount each month.

So, what categories should you include in your everyday expenses? This should cover every category that your family spends money on that is not a set amount — that is, not a bill or a direct debit. So it will include the same categories that I named above for cash budgeting: groceries, fuel, personal spending, clothing or kids' activities, for example. Choose the categories that will suit you and your family best. It's important to remember that you do not have to put money into every category, every paycheque. Some months you may not need to put money into clothing, for example. The amounts that you budget in each category may also vary from month to month.

It is also extremely important to budget for fun things, as well as personal spending money for your whole family. These categories are what will help keep you to your budget. If the budget is too strict, you won't stick to it, and you'll be more likely to rebel. Use the money from these categories on experiences such as a coffee with friends or a family outing — even that pair of shoes you've been eyeing up. I recommend budgeting your own personal money and that of your partner separately; this is money that you can spend or save, without having to justify the decision to each other or stressing about whatever you do spend. The same goes for your children, if you have any; we'll come back to this, but I advise encouraging them to earn pocket or spending money from the age of about six.

We'll return to both everyday expenses and cash budgeting in the worksheet section, where you will make a note of the amount you are planning to spend in each category (regardless of whether you are cash budgeting or not).

Budgeting by paycheque

You are going to make a budget for each paycheque. Working to relatively short timeframes gives you the chance to reset and adjust any parts of your budget that may need tweaking. Did you have enough budgeted in each category? Do you have any money left in a particular category at the end of the period? If so, should you budget a little less to that area from your next paycheque?

How often you create a budget therefore depends on how often you get paid. Paid monthly? Create a monthly budget. If you're paid weekly, you'll be making a budget every week. I've added five budget sheets for every month, which you can find in the worksheets later in the book. This means that, no matter how often you are paid, you'll have space to create a budget for each paycheque. Each budget is centred on your paycheque, meaning that you can create a budget unique to the income that you will receive and the expenses that are due within that period.

What happens if you have more than one job, or receive income from something you do in your spare time? If this income is expected, then it should be planned for – that is, included in a budget. Say you get paid for your main job on 6 June, but you also work part time and will be paid for this on 8 June. Well, then your budget for 6 June should also include the income from 8 June. If you receive unexpected income, however – say, from selling an item second hand – then I recommend budgeting that money into your next paycheque. Put whatever you've made somewhere safe, so that you aren't tempted to spend it before it is budgeted, and then include it in your next budget.

Since you're budgeting by paycheque, this can look very different depending on whether you're paid monthly or paid weekly. If you are paid monthly, you may have to leave larger amounts in your account to pay your rent or mortgage. From my experience, two big tips when budgeting a monthly income would be:

- Where possible, request that bills and direct debits be paid on a date close to your payday, including your rent or mortgage. This just makes everything a little less stressful.
- Try acting as though you get paid twice in the month. Divide the total amount you intend to spend on your everyday expenses in half. Then take that amount out in cash when you first get paid, so that you aren't overwhelmed or tempted to spend the full total. You can withdraw the rest in the second half of the month.

Variable income

If your exact income is not known, plan your budget around your *expected* income. If this varies with each paycheque – if your income comes from a small business, for example, or is commission-based – then base your budget on a low estimate. If the actual amount that comes in is higher than you have prepared for, you can update your budget – this may be an opportunity to send extra towards your savings or debt. Do not let it just sit in your account without a job: I guarantee it will disappear.

Variable income can be a little trickier to budget at first, especially with a new business or if your income is dependent on meeting targets. It will be easier over time, however – both as you become more experienced with budgeting and as you have more months of income for comparison. You'll be able to look at your past income alongside your expenses, and it will become easier to predict your future paycheques.

Many find that if their income is vastly variable, it can be useful to get one month ahead on their bills. You can keep this money with your emergency fund (in addition to that €1,000). Then, if your income is drastically lower one month, at least you know that your bills are covered, giving you time to sort out your income situation. I strongly recommend not leaving this money in your main bank account, though, as it can be harder to track what money is for current bills and what you have set aside for the future … as well as the obvious temptation to spend it on other things!

Starting to budget

STEP ONE

So, the very first thing that I recommend you do is to look back at your last month. Print out that statement, grab a few highlighters and start figuring out where your money went. Divide your outgoings into categories – these can be bills, fuel, that cheeky coffee … everything! – using a different colour for each category if possible, and start making a note of what you spent where. Keep a note of this list, because believe me, once you get started on this journey, you'll be amazed to look back at your initial spending habits!

Personally, I was afraid of this step the first time I started budgeting. I definitely had my head in the sand, and I didn't really want to know where I was spending unnecessarily! I recommend checking in on your bank account regularly, just to make sure everything is going as it should ... Back before I took control of my financial habits, I would sometimes get direct debits bouncing and I had such a feeling of dread before this step. However, it is so important! Without looking back, you cannot move forwards; you have no foundations to base your budget on. The numbers that you have written down will show you areas that you may be overspending in, and they'll guide you when writing your first budget.

Step two

The next step is to write a list of all your direct debits, bills and standing orders. You can list these later in this book, where there's a dedicated bills and direct debits section. I recommend listing them in order of the date that they come out of your account, as this makes them easier to read later. Write down the dates that each one is coming out and the amount that will be due. If the amount varies, write the highest possible amount.

Once you have written this list, you may find that there are subscriptions and direct debits for services that you no longer use or really need. This is one area where you may be able to reduce your spending. Even if you don't want to cancel a service, you may still be able to get a better deal by switching providers, switching plans or even ringing your provider to see if they can offer anything better.

Step three

Next, you need to list any large annual expenses that you have coming up, when these are due and the total amount. For each of these you'll make a sinking fund, which means that these large and financially stressful costs become much more manageable.

While I recommend listing all the large expenses that you are expecting over the next year, ideally, you'll only work on five to seven sinking funds at a time. This is because you will struggle to reach your sinking-fund goals if you have too many – you'll be adding smaller amounts, as the total will have to be split across more funds. It may also as overwhelming to keep track of your sinking funds if you have more than seven. Of course, once you have completed a sinking fund, you can then replace this with another sinking fund, but by sticking to a restricted number at one time, you are prioritising the expenses that you need to save for. We'll look at this in more detail in the next section, but you can either divide and conquer your sinking funds – in which case, you divide the total amount by the number of months left until that amount is due – or you can pay by priority, focussing on the costs that are coming up first. That's grand too.

STEP FOUR

Now that you're beginning to understand your starting figures, it's time to set some financial goals. What would you like to achieve in the next six months? Try to come up with at least three manageable goals. Include your partner and family, as this will affect them too, and the process will always be easier when you work as a team. Make sure that your goals have a measurable result, so that you know when you have achieved them! Examples of solid financial goals might include getting your emergency fund up to €1,000, putting a certain amount towards your debt or a large sinking fund, or increasing your income by a certain figure.

You can also add goals for one year's time and five years' time. These may seem very large right now, but as you take control of your finances, you'll realise that they're more achievable than you think. As a way of helping you to visualise your five-year goals, I recommend writing down your perfect day. In an ideal world, what would a day in your life look like in five years' time? What job will you have (and what are you being paid), where do you live, what are your hobbies – even what car do you drive? You'll be able to see what motivates you; the details you include here are the parts of your life that are most important to you. I've also included space to create a vision board, as you may prefer to use images to remind yourself exactly what you're aiming to achieve!

STEP FIVE

Before starting your budget, go and mark your paydays in the 'Your month at a glance' calendar. Then add in all the bills that are due that month, writing in the name of the bill and the amount to be paid on the day that the bill is due.

Then get your highlighters out again and circle the payday in a certain colour – and then highlight all the bills that will be paid with that paycheque in the same colour. This way, you'll be able to identify at a glance which paycheque will cover which bills. There is also room below the calendar to total the bills for each paycheque, which is helpful when writing your budget.

STEP SIX

Now that you've put the groundwork in, it's time for an exciting step: you're going to start your budget! I find that the best time to write this is a day or two before payday. That way you're prepared before the money hits; your plan will be in place, and you won't be tempted to spend your income on areas that you haven't allowed for.

Name your budget

First, you're going to name your budget. This is important for looking back, so that you will know exactly what paycheque this is centred on. If you have several incomes listed on this budget, always name it after your primary income – 'First paycheque in May', for example.

List your income

Next, list all your income for this paycheque, including side hustles, income left over from your last budget and even gifted income. List the income details, the date it was or will be paid and the amount. Then total your overall income.

After this, you need to list any bills and direct debits that are due in this period. To do so, simply go to your calendar, find your highlighted pay period and all the bills that are highlighted in the same colour. Enter these into your budget. I like to then total the bills and round up to the nearest €10. As a cash budgeter, this makes sense, as I can only take notes out of my account. I also like to leave that little bit extra in the bank as a very small buffer. This can come in handy if a bill is slightly larger than I expected or if I've forgotten that a bill was going to increase.

Cash envelopes

Next up are your cash envelopes – or your 'virtual envelopes' if you are not going to cash budget. This category includes all your everyday spending. In step one, you'll have identified the categories that you spend in. I like to budget these categories in order of importance, so that the necessities are taken care of first.

I'm always asked 'how do you know how much to budget?' This is why we looked back at our last month's spending. So, say that as a family you spent €1,200 on groceries in the last month. Well, bearing in mind that you will hopefully be more intentional with your spending this month, it wouldn't be totally unrealistic to assume that a budget of €100 less than this would be achievable. Remember, the amount you are budgeting for has to last until your next paycheque, so if you spend everything in the first week, the rest of the month will be tricky … You should also keep in mind that you'll be using notes for your cash envelopes, so will want to keep your figures round. I like to keep my envelopes mostly in €10 notes, as I find it harder to find places where I can withdraw €5 notes.

It usually takes about three months for people to get to a good place with their budget and start using accurate figures. So go easy on yourself and don't give up after the first month – that one in particular is a total estimate and you're more than likely to be slightly off in a few categories. And of course, you can jiggle the envelopes around to make your money last to the next paycheque. Even a seasoned budgeter like myself may need to do this from time to time.

Sinking funds

Next, it's time to put some money aside for future expenses. We'll look at sinking funds in more detail in the next section, and the different methods that you can use to save towards them, but this is the point at which you'll put some of your income towards expenses that you know are coming, such as birthdays or Christmas, so that when they arrive, that month's income won't take such a hit.

Financial goals

If you haven't already started, this is where you are going to work on saving your emergency fund. This goes into the savings section of your budget. Yes, I know that if you have some debt you'll be eager to start chipping away at that, but without an emergency fund, your budget may be at risk.

Once your emergency fund is complete, it's time to work on your next goal. *Now* you'll start to work on paying off any debt, and I'll address the methods you can use to chip away at this later in this section. If you've already cleared your debt, or you are working on other savings, you can add this figure into your savings. You can certainly work on a savings goal while also paying off debt, but it will slow your progress.

This is why goal-setting is so important. You're in charge of your budget, and you can re-evaluate your goals any time you want. I think you're much better taking a little longer to pay off your debt because you're saving to buy a second-hand car than adding to your debt by taking out a new loan to cover the purchase.

Summary

This is where you will quickly make sure that your income minus your expenses equals zero, to complete your zero-based budget. Take a moment to look over your figures and make sure that you're happy with everything.

STEP SEVEN

The final step is your payday routine. As soon as you've been paid, check your bank account and make sure that your income matches the amount that you budgeted for. Remember, the budget you created before payday was just a plan. Plans can change, and if you receive more income or less, take a moment to adjust your budget as you need to. (There's no better feeling than adjusting your budget for an increased income – this is your chance to send more money towards those financial goals!)

Once you have checked your income, it's time to put your money to work. Using your budget, leave the amount needed for bills and direct debits in your accounts. Next, take out the cash you need to stuff your envelopes, or transfer the money digitally if you're using online pots. Finally, send the remainder of your paycheque to your final goals. You've covered all your bills and essentials, and now it's time to put money towards changing your financial future!

Getting your partner on board

So, you've discovered this amazing way of looking after your finances and taking control ... but how do you bring your partner round to the idea? I get asked this question a lot. For those of you in relationships, communication is going to be a massive factor here – because making these kinds of big financial decisions is going to impact your life, and will affect your partner too. You can't just say 'I found this woman, Caz, and she's written a book telling people how to budget your money – so that's what we're going to do and that's that!' It would be treating your partner like a child; anyone I know would be likely to shut down. In reading this book so far, you have already started on a journey; you've been open to the idea of change. Now you are ready to take some information on board and to start overhauling some areas of your life. It's important that you allow your partner the same journey.

The first thing that I would suggest doing is to sit down with your partner and talk through your concerns about the current family finances. Try to keep the conversation light but be clear about the points that you struggle with. You may be surprised – they might share your concerns ... alternatively, it may be a surprise to them that this has even occurred to you, especially if they've had their head in the sand. The conversation may then naturally turn to looking for a solution, to taking back control, and that's when you could introduce them to these principles. Such ideas could be completely new to your partner, so don't expect them to get overly excited; they may be sceptical.

If the conversation doesn't turn towards solutions, don't despair – they may just need some time to think the conversation over. I'm married to a thinker and it's just how they problem-solve. Instead, wait a little while and then bring the conversation back up, asking them if they've thought any more about the situation.

It may be helpful to frame the change as temporary, an experiment. Let's try to budget our finances. Let's follow all the steps and find out where our money is going. We should try to reduce our spending in some areas, and we may need to think about what we want to work towards financially. Let's give ourselves a deadline and make it manageable – three months. Let's track our spending, plan our budget; everything for three months. If we don't notice a difference to our finances in that time, then we know we gave it our best shot. Three months!

Hopefully this chat will really help. Something else you may want to think about – and identify – is that there are often spenders and savers in a relationship. Neither is better, and both can cause issues when budgeting. A spender, obviously, is liable to overspend money; this may be caused by emotions, impulses or deeper issues. They may not even realise that they are the spender. When trying to take control of your finances, it's important, if you are a spender, to reduce the triggers for your spending: unsubscribe from email marketing lists, remove yourself from bargain-finding groups, delete those websites that you have bookmarked in your browser – anything to reduce the temptation. And don't forget, cash may be your best friend for this issue. It's much harder to impulse-buy with cash, that's for sure!

A saver, meanwhile, will struggle with other aspects of budgeting. They won't like the idea of overpaying debt … They'll likely feel uncomfortable handing over that money, and may suggest just saving it instead. They may also struggle with trusting the spender to budget their money effectively.

Of course, you may find that you have a mixture of spender and saver in both you and your partner. The important thing is to understand **why** you sometimes self-sabotage with your financial choices, and think about how you both are going to work towards preventing those triggers from affecting your budget.

Now … what do you do if the big chat hasn't helped – if, despite your best efforts, your partner still doesn't want to know? It is so, so important in the long term that you do both get on the same page. You cannot force someone to change. But something that worked well for me, when I was hoping to get my husband on board, was to show him the results from budgeting.

I budgeted my finances and started saving for future expenses. At the time, I was saving a good bit towards car expenses in a sinking fund, as my old car was on its last legs (or wheels!). Anyway, one day my car just completely broke down. Massive repairs were needed and my husband was getting extremely stressed – until I explained that it was fine, that I had almost the full amount saved. We were able to find the remainder, and the experience completely proved the importance of that sinking fund. The following week, without any further discussion about it, my husband approached me and asked for help. He wanted to start a budget and to start his own sinking funds as well. He had seen the impact of my budgeting first hand and realised that it would really benefit his finances too. Sometimes you just need to give a reluctant partner a little time and they will see the results for themselves.

Introducing your children to budgeting

We sat our kids down and explained our finances to them at the end of 2018. Our children were aged seven and ten, and we sat them down and told them that we were about to embark on a low-spend year. This was a life-changing moment for our family, and as a parent, it was a moment that my husband and I found very hard. I'll look more closely at the concept of a low-spend year later in this book, but essentially it involves a complete change in your spending habits for a set amount of time, in order to achieve a financial goal.

In our case, we explained to our children that we would be spending less on everything that wasn't essential, in order to be in a position to own our own home. It was important to us that they understood that we would still being having fun, meeting friends and making memories – just in ways that cost very little money.

Our children took it very well, and I think this was mostly because we were very open with them. We told them about our credit-card debt, and how we were worried about it, and so our first goal was to pay that off. We told them how much we hoped to save each month and our overall plan. Probably the most important thing we told them was the end date: no matter how things went, we would finish our low-spend year at the end of the year. My only regret is not being so open sooner, as the gift of knowing how to manage their own money has been one of the greatest things we have been able to give our children.

Children can be introduced to the basics of budgeting from about the age of six or seven. They're like sponges – you'll probably be surprised how quickly they pick it up. This is a great time to introduce pocket money, if you haven't already. We give our children chore charts: they have jobs that they must do that aren't monetised – that just generally help the house to run, help the family – but we also list a few jobs that they can do to earn some money. I don't try to force them to do these jobs; it's completely up to the kids whether they decide to do them. I choose jobs that are relative to their age – a 7-year-old will have very different abilities to a 12-year-old. There should be a mixture of jobs on the list, some easy and some that take a little more time. Then, once you have set your jobs, you need to decide how much you are going to give your child per job completed. Two things to bear in mind when setting your 'prices':

- You need to make sure that it is an amount that your budget can afford. This is so, so important, because you need to be consistent and pay on time. When you make a deal with a child, they expect to be rewarded when they complete a task. You can, of course, pay once a week, but they won't take an IOU!
- The amount paid will likely have to increase as the child grows. A large amount of money for a six-year-old won't go as far for a teenager – and just as in the real world, it can be beneficial to give pay rises as your children's experience and responsibilities grow. If you start the chore payment price too high now, you'll struggle later.

I ask my children to then budget their income and divide it into 'spend' and 'save'. A certain amount is put towards longer-term savings, and they can choose to spend the remainder on whatever they wish. This is teaching them about short- and long-term goals, as well as being in control of their own money. Yes, there will be times they spend it all on sweeties or stuff they don't need, but it's all a learning experience!

Another bonus to giving your children an earned income is that, instead of having to say no to everything they want, you can redirect the question. Encourage your kids to understand that this is something they would have to pay for themselves, and so they need to decide for themselves if they would like to buy it. If they do, then they have less to spend next time — simple. Just like us, they'll quickly learn the value of saving for a more valuable item.

Once kids in your life have a basic understanding of budgeting their own money, they'll also start to notice how you budget *your* money. It's so important that you share your own financial goals and journey with your children. When I talk about changing your financial future, this is the bigger picture: hopefully changing your family's finances across generations.

We have been sharing our own journey with our children for years; they journeyed alongside us through the year we saved for our house deposit and celebrated when we got the keys. They have watched us clear debt, change incomes and save towards our goals. In turn, my son recently bought a gaming PC with money that he had saved all by himself. He researched every aspect, learned how to build the PC and then waited patiently for the parts to arrive. It was such a proud moment for me to watch him open the boxes!

Savings

Emergency funds

As I said earlier, an emergency fund, also known as a rainy-day fund, is the first goal that I want you to work towards. You need an emergency fund of at least a few hundred euro, and ideally you should be working towards €1,000 in your emergency fund. Yes, this can seem like a lot of money, especially when your finances are tight, but its importance cannot be underestimated!

Given that it is so crucial, I recommend recording your emergency-fund total in your savings tracker, which can be found in the worksheets later in the book. That way, when you look back at your year, you'll be able to see at a glance how much you saved each month towards this goal. There is also a space for your savings goals in each budget, and this is where you should make a note of any money that is going towards your emergency fund from each paycheque. I've also added a visual tracker that you can fill in as you add to your fund.

An emergency fund – or the absence of one – can 100 per cent change your family's finances. Instead of turning to debt or trying to cash flow an emergency, and then struggling later, you'll be able to continue as you were doing without diverting funds from your other financial priorities, and continue to get closer to your goals.

Why do I recommend €1,000 in your emergency fund? Well, that amount would cover most families in most immediate scenarios, but if your family needs a bit more to be covered, go for it. Homeowners may also consider beefing their emergency fund up a little (once they have reached some of their bigger financial goals), so that they have enough to cover a few of these larger financial emergencies. Because unfortunately, unexpected house-related costs might not happen alone – a leak in the ceiling can lead to replastering or new carpets, for example. Once you have an emergency fund saved that works for you, then you can begin to attack your debt, save for your house deposit or work towards whatever your particular goal is.

So, what is a financial emergency?

A financial emergency is a sudden, unexpected cost that urgently needs to be paid. Examples of financial emergencies include medical costs, your car breaking down, a household repair or a sudden loss of earnings – and these are what your emergency fund is set up to cover. The money in your fund should be saved in an account that is separate from your main bank account and easy to access in an emergency … but not *too* easy to access. You don't want to be tempted to 'borrow' from it for that pair of shoes on sale! It is so important that you start saving into an emergency fund as soon as you can because it can take a while to build up, and of course there's no way of knowing when that money will be needed.

If you do have to use your emergency fund, don't panic – that's exactly what it's there for. It is there to turn a crisis into an inconvenience! You won't want to spend it, but you'll be annoyed about the loss of savings rather than stressed about actually finding the money, and when dealing with a financial emergency, the last thing you need is added stress. Having that money in place will just give your finances a safety net and help ease any worries about the unexpected. So, it's truly not a problem to use your emergency fund if and when you need it – but just don't forget to build it back up as soon as you can.

Sinking funds

Sinking funds are where you save small amounts over time towards a big expense that you know is coming. It's a specific goal, and usually due on a certain date. Sinking funds can include things like Christmas, birthdays, back-to-school costs and holidays. You should start saving towards these expenses from your first budget. They are usually large and, by starting to save for them as far in advance as you can, you'll take away the stress of having to find a way of paying for them. I would highly recommend that you work on five to seven sinking funds at a time. There's a space within each budget for you to track your sinking funds.

The beauty of a sinking fund is that when the expense is due, instead of feeling stressed out, you'll already have that money there, set aside. By saving towards these costs over time, you are breaking the expense into much more manageable chunks. Also, by preparing for an expense that you know is coming, you will be less likely to turn towards debt to cover it. That feeling when you have the money there, the moment the amount is due, is honestly the best peace of mind. I remember the first Christmas sinking fund I had – that feeling of going shopping for gifts, knowing that the money was there, was amazing; plus it made the post-Christmas period so much easier to manage!

So, how do you decide how much to put towards sinking funds each month?

There are two different methods of saving towards these future expenses: division and priority.

Division saving is when you divide the total amount due by the months that are left between now and the due date. That amount is the total you would need to set aside each month to reach your goal. This method can be automated, so it's great for busy people who don't want to think about this calculation every month; you can set up a standing order to send the monthly total for your sinking funds into a specific savings account. Division saving can be difficult if your income fluctuates, however, or if you have other expenses that are due soon.

Priority saving is when you save towards the sinking funds that are most important and/or due next. This is the method I use – so, for example, saving towards back-to-school over the summer, towards Christmas in the autumn and for birthdays throughout the year. This system takes a little more planning, and you'll need to make sure that you don't forget events and occasions. (I've included a section in this book to help you keep on top of them!) This way of saving can great for lower incomes, as there is a little more flexibility. It's also great for people who are more motivated to save towards expenses that are coming soon rather than those that are the best part of a year away. It doesn't mean completely ignoring all your other sinking funds, however; I recommend saving more towards your prioritised funds, but also putting a little towards your other categories. This just allows you to get a bit of a head start on those other funds, no matter how small – and when you come to focus on those goals, the idea of completing them won't feel as overwhelming.

Where should you save this money?

So, while I am a cash budgeter – and some fellow cash budgeters will save their sinking funds in cash – I've found that, as the amounts saved increased, it was no longer practical to save my sinking funds in cash. If it's something that works well for you, however, then it's certainly an option.

An alternative approach is to group all your sinking funds together in a savings account. This account should be easily accessible, and ideally online transfers should be possible for ease. The downside to this option is that all your money for various sinking funds is together, so it's important to be very organised and disciplined. It would be easy to overspend your budget for something like Christmas, leaving another sinking fund short.

Finally, another method is to save your sinking funds in a bank account that allows you to use named saving pots. As we spoke about in the cash budgeting section, these become like virtual envelopes that you can easily save into. This is the option that my husband and I use, and we find it so helpful. I like that you can set targets, which is a great visual tool for keeping me motivated!

Debt

Dealing with debt

Debt is extremely common these days, but that doesn't mean it should be normal. We are living in a society where everyone is told to have the newest technology, drive a certain car or wear clothes with certain labels. These things are marketed to us day and night – on ads, on social media, even via product placement in films. And part of the problem is that debt is now easier than ever to obtain; alongside the bombardment of things we can buy to achieve a lifestyle we aspire to, there is also easy access to credit … you can apply online and be approved in minutes – it's terrifying, really!

Years ago, you would have had to think about a purchase in a shop and find the money to buy it. If you didn't have the money, you would have had to leave and go to a lender, or save. You would have had lots of time to think about the purchase. Nowadays, you can be tempted by an item online, follow the link with one click, and if you don't have enough money to purchase it, many sites will immediately offer finance, both through store credit and outside providers. If you are paying for a product or service using any kind of 'buy now, pay later' or 'pay in interest-free payments' button, this is debt. There is no grey area; this is money that you owe. It is debt. You can literally obtain debt in minutes – without leaving your chair, without mulling it over, without thinking about the consequences.

But don't worry if you recognise yourself in this behaviour, because now is the time to form a plan: we are going to tackle that debt! I know it can feel overwhelming, especially if you have multiple debts, but I'm going to talk you through two great methods for clearing your debt.

Ultimately, you want to break the debt cycle. My family and I were in this cycle ourselves – where we cleared debt only to get more. For us, it was car loans; we'd clear one five-year loan, but then it would be time to replace the car and get another five-year loan. It was only when we set ourselves up for success that we were able to break that cycle.

First, you must set up your emergency fund. We've talked about the importance of this fund in general already, but it's particularly tied to debt, since debt is what many of us turn to in times of crisis. Turning to debt in a monetary emergency, when you are not thinking about repayments or cost, is never going to be a good financial decision. If you have your emergency fund ready and waiting, however, it won't even occur to you to use debt.

Your second step should be to save now for future expenses. Christmas happens every year, same day, yet many people panic in October or November about not having enough to cover the costs … and again turn to debt. And it's the same with holidays: they're expensive – even a budget holiday can be financially overwhelming and a small loan may feel justified. Again, we've already discussed how to avoid this minefield: sinking funds! You're going to start saving little and often for those big costs, so that they don't hit quite so hard when they come.

So far, all things that we've already learned. But now let's look at actually tackling whatever debt you have. First things first: you need to check that you will not be penalised for paying off your debt early. If you have a few debts, check the small print on each one to make sure that you won't be charged for closing that debt before the term ends. Most places will not charge you, but some may. Even if you are going to be charged, early repayment may still be worth doing … as the penalty charge may be less than the total amount you would pay if you just continued making the minimum payments.

Now, there are two methods for paying off debt. With both methods you will still be paying the minimum payment on *all* of your debts, while throwing extra payments at the debt you are prioritising (the difference is that which debt is prioritised depends on which method you've chosen to follow). Once you have cleared your first debt through its minimum payment *plus* extra payments, you can then put that total amount towards your next debt – along with *its* minimum payment. I've always found that clearing that first debt really motivates you and boosts your momentum towards clearing the next one!

Snowball method

For the snowball method, you are going to list your debts – from the smallest amount to the biggest – and you're going to chip away at the smallest debt first. You are paying the minimum payment on all of your debts, but this smallest debt is getting its minimum payment *plus an overpayment*.

You keep overpaying that lowest debt – while continuing to pay the minimum payments on all others – until that debt is gone. Then you move on to the second-smallest debt, and your payment for this will be its minimum payment plus the money you're no longer paying to the smallest debt – that is, the first debt's minimum payment plus its overpayment. The second debt is therefore getting even more of an overpayment that the first debt; it's just like rolling a snowball, picking up speed and gathering momentum as it goes. Personally, I find this method motivating, as you will clear your smallest debts first (often reasonably quickly), and by the time you get to your largest debt you will be throwing the most money at it.

Avalanche method

For this method, you ignore the total amounts of your debts and instead list them in order of interest amount. Then, you overpay the debt with the highest interest rate first, working your way down to the debt with the lowest interest rate. As with the snowball method, you must still continue to pay the minimum payments on all your other debts.

This method usually saves you money overall, as you will be paying less interest; however, it can feel less motivating than the snowball method, as the debt that is charging you the most interest could be a larger debt and so may take a while to clear.

Some people find that a combination of both methods works well – for example, using the snowball method at first and knocking out a few of the smaller debts to build motivation, and then moving to the avalanche method.

When clearing debts, the most important thing is to keep chipping away. Even if you feel that your overpayment isn't significant, it all adds up. Every overpayment is a step closer to losing those payments altogether, and freeing up more income in your budget to put towards exciting financial goals!

Lifestyle creep

Lifestyle creep is where you receive an increase in your household income and your spending increases as a result. Usually this is very gradual (hence the 'creep'); it happens over time and you often won't notice until the change becomes significant. And no matter how budget-conscious or frugal you may be, it can happen to anyone. It absolutely happened to us!

When my middle child started school, I went back to college for a year and retrained. This was difficult financially, but we were excited to become a two-income household after many years on a single wage. I was lucky enough to start working before my course finished, and we began to budget the two incomes.

For the first year, we were still very careful. We had to buy a new car soon after I started, and we were paying for that, but that was about all. I would say that our lifestyle creep must have started about halfway through my second year of working – as I've noted above, it's hard to pinpoint the exact moment! I would say it started with buying items online. I love a new pair of trainers, and would justify the purchase by telling myself that I needed them for work. Similarly, we gradually began eating out more, spending more on groceries than we should have and basically having no plan for our money. I had no idea then, but lifestyle creep had truly taken hold already!

Then, as we went into the next year, we booked a family holiday abroad for the summer. Although we did save for that holiday, we didn't save for the second holiday we booked that year. The second holiday was to America, and all spending while there – including car rental, a new phone, eating out, everything – went straight on the credit card. We had a ball!

However, the moment that credit-card bill came through the post, I got a feeling of dread that I will never forget. We had known it would be big, and we'd even talked about our spending on the flight home, but ultimately, we'd sort of stuck our heads in the sand, refusing to acknowledge how bad the problem could be. But when that bill came through the door, we realised that we were in trouble if we didn't do something about this debt ...

That was the moment we completely changed our mindset and started to take control. Maybe now, as you read these words, you are reaching this moment yourself. By keeping to a budget, even as your income increases, you will be able to prevent lifestyle creep.

Increasing debt

If debt isn't good, what about a mortgage? It's a question I've been asked before, and most of us will need to take out a mortgage at some point in our lives. I will not be the person to tell you that this is 'good' debt; if you had the cash in the bank, my personal advice would be to use that! Honestly, though, for most of us, the only way we will ever own our own home is by saving up a deposit and signing on the dotted line for a mortgage.

Early mortgage pay-off is a goal that many people will work towards once all their other debt is paid off. This is a decision that will depend on you and your budget. For many, paying off their mortgage early is an emotionally motivated decision that will give a great feeling of relief, as well as the obvious bonus of that mortgage payment no longer leaving their bank account.

The reason why many others do not prioritise paying off their mortgage early is because they may be leaving themselves with less money to put towards retirement, college for their kids, future expenses, investing — even generally a greater quality of life. For our family, it is not a goal that we are going to work towards any time soon, simply because we have other goals that we feel are more important right now. We want to save a larger emergency fund first, and then we will be investing in our future. It's a decision that is unique to every family, but an important decision that is definitely due consideration once your mortgage is your only debt.

In terms of acquiring a mortgage, if you are going to be applying for one in the near future, my best advice is to try and get as small a mortgage as you can and to opt for a shorter term — such as a 15-year mortgage rather than one for 30 years – if you can afford to. Buying more house than you can afford will make it harder for you to have enough income left for your other financial goals after that mortgage is paid!

We were very conscious of the size of our mortgage when we were looking to buy. We ended up buying a house that needed a little work in another county from where we had been living. It was important to us that we would always be able to afford the mortgage repayments.

And although it's far from ideal, there are a few rare, other circumstances when you may need to consider adding to your debt. What sort of circumstances? Well, sometimes it can be useful to consolidate your debts into one lower-interest loan. This could save you money, but I would only recommend doing this once you have been budgeting for a while and have already started knocking those debts out. This is because it's much more motivating to be paying off multiple debts. Another instance could be if an expense cropped up that was higher than your €1,000 emergency fund – the boiler needing replaced, for example, or a big medical cost that you couldn't foresee. If the expense is absolutely necessary for your family, then of course you have to incur more debt – but it's helpful to really interrogate your use of the phrase 'absolutely necessary'. I've often classed something as essential, only to later find a way around the expense or to reduce it, so if you can take a few days to think about it, do. Above all, the important thing to remember is that you are now in control of your finances. Even if you find yourself in a situation where it is necessary to take on more debt, you will have the tools to clear that debt as fast as you can and get back to working on other financial goals.

Making your money stretch

Saving money on your food shop

An area where many people overspend is on their food shop. Certainly, this was an area where we really found some savings once we started to look. Below are some of the tips and tricks we used, which helped up to reduce our weekly food shop spend from €250 to €100, including nappies, cleaning products and toiletries (and despite adding another family member!).

CHECK THE FRIDGE, FREEZER AND CUPBOARDS

Often you'll already have ingredients at home that could make a meal; perhaps you're only missing one item. Put that item alone on the shopping list, rather than running through the whole recipe and buying more of things that you already have. This is also a good chance to see if there are any pantry staples that you need to restock, such as items needed for breakfasts or lunches for the week.

CREATE A MEAL PLAN

Start with the meals you already have that need to be eaten, or ones you found the ingredients for when looking through the cupboards. You don't need to stick to a strict order for your meal plan; you may find deals or reduced items during your food shop that need to be eaten earlier in the week – or you might simply not fancy Bolognese on Monday in the end! Keep it simple and flexible, and then it'll be more likely to work.

LOOK AT WEEKLY OFFERS AND SPECIALS

Before you make your grocery list, look online and check supermarket brochures or apps. There are usually fruit and vegetable offers, as well as meat and poultry deals. Look at all of the offers and see if they will work well for your family; if they will, use them in your meal plan. Pop those ingredients on your grocery list. This will also help you to decide where you will be doing your grocery shop this week.

Make that list!

This is so, so important. This is your plan; without it, you'll forget items or buy stuff that you don't need. Personally, I know it was always when I went to the shop without a list that I found myself wandering the aisles and throwing items into the trolley that had caught my eye. There was no plan, and we often went way over budget. Plan for a whole week's groceries: fewer trips to the supermarket mean less chance for you to overspend. You may need a small top-up shop for perishables such as milk and bread, but try and keep it to only a few items – those multiple trips will really up your spend.

Set your budget and stick to it

This is where bringing a certain amount in cash can really help so much. If you only have that amount with you, then you can't go over budget (and nobody enjoys putting stuff back). If you don't want to use cash, use an online savings pot and stick strictly to the amount you have in there.

Know your grocery costs before you get to the till

This ties in nicely with the last point. If you have a budget, this is how you stick to it. There won't be any surprises and you'll make better decisions as you shop because your total will be adding up and impulse purchases will leave less room for the items on your list. Some people can have a good estimate in their head before they get to the till, but don't be afraid to properly calculate your shop as you go if mental maths isn't your strong suit.

STORE YOUR FOOD PROPERLY ONCE YOU GET HOME

So much food is wasted every year due to incorrect storage. Make full use of your freezer; many more items can be frozen than you might think. Most meat can be frozen and can be defrosted overnight in the bottom of the fridge. I like to leave enough meat fresh from the food shop for a maximum of two or three dinners, and then freeze the rest. Portion this into different meals — if they will make more than one meal — and write the date you're freezing them on the packet. And whatever you're freezing, just make sure you add it to your monthly freezer inventory. This is especially important if you own a chest freezer, as it can be so much harder to see what food is there in the bottom. Fruit should be placed in containers that reduce spoiling and stored in the fridge. I like to use containers that are clear so that their contents are easy to see and reach for, and store the snacks that aren't as fresh or as healthy out of sight.

I go through the above steps every time I do a food shop. It may seem like a lot at first, but it'll quickly become second nature and will save you so much money in the long run! Here are a few small final tips that will really help you to make the most of your food shop:

- Leave the kids at home — maybe even your partner too if they struggle to stick to the budget!
- Choose a quieter time to shop; you'll feel less stressed and will be more likely to keep to your plan.
- Make sure you know where reduced-sticker items are found in the shop. Midweek is a great time to score these, or just before a bank holiday, and the greatest reductions are usually an hour or two before closing.
- And we've all heard it: do not shop on an empty stomach.

Saving money with your meals

Some of my most popular money-saving features are my 'feeding five people for €5' videos on Instagram and TikTok — but my family doesn't eat these meals daily. We eat a wide variety of meals and that may often work out cheaper than

€5 per meal, because we use leftovers a lot. I like to batch cook, often creating meals that I can dump into the slow cooker on busy days, or ones that use items that were reduced or part of special offers in the supermarket.

I also rarely buy jars of sauce; most sauces are cheaper when made from scratch – not to mention heathier, because you know what is in them! A simple white sauce, for example, contains just butter or oil, flour, milk and some seasoning, and then this can be used in lasagne, mac and cheese or even a fish pie.

Another way to save money on your food shop is by staying versatile with your ingredients. For example, if you make a stew in November, it will likely have very different ingredients to a stew made in May, as there will be different vegetables in season. And don't be afraid to buy frozen vegetables and use them instead of fresh. They are often as healthy, if not even more packed with vitamins and minerals, as they are picked and frozen almost straight away, whereas the fresh broccoli on the shelf will be slowly losing its nutrients each day.

I like to also freeze prepped meals, vegetables, fruit and meat. Chopping onions can seem like a chore when you're stuck for time, so I like to cut extra portions any time I do have the chopping board out. The extra diced onions can then be thrown into the freezer, and that step is complete for the next meal. Portioning out and freezing meat, as I already mentioned in relation to food waste, saves time and money also.

If your family is anything like mine, you'll have a few favourite recipes that you return to again and again. I find it helpful to look for new inspiration regularly, and advise aiming to have a mixture of meals that your family enjoys that may take a bit of time to prepare, along with meals that can be thrown together in a hurry. These quick meals are going to be the ones you turn to in a pinch or on the nights that you just don't fancy cooking. Knowing that you have something tasty, but simple, that you can whip up will save you from getting that takeaway that you hadn't planned on having. And of course, tried and tested doesn't have to mean boring. You can mix things up by trying different cuts of meat or different vegetables with a meal. This can save you so much money – as you can opt for whatever's on offer – and you can often cook the meat a different way to achieve the same or similar result.

You can use extra vegetables, beans and other pulses to increase the volume of a meal and make it more filling. I find that using red lentils in a chilli works really well, for example, as does adding lots of beans and additional vegetables. Bulking out your recipes in this way can help create leftovers for the next day or stretch a meal to feed a larger family.

You can also look to save money on the way that you make your food. Smaller kitchen appliances are usually cheaper to run than using the oven or the hob. Having your slow cooker, for example, on for eight hours on the low setting costs less than half the price of having the oven on for just one hour. It's the same with air fryers, pressure cookers, soup makers, etc., so do aim to make use of these appliances if you have them!

In-store versus online shopping

Nowadays we have more choice than ever as to how we get our groceries, but the main difference is whether we choose to go into a shop or order items online. I find that the main method you use depends entirely on your schedule — how much time you have to shop — and general preference.

With online shopping, you have a choice between click and collect and delivery. The former involves selecting your groceries online and then arranging to pick them up at a certain time, while delivery — well, there's the same pre-selection but then the items are (of course!) delivered to you. Both of these options are convenient and time saving, but do they save you money?

Well, the delivery service has a fee. This varies according to the time of day and how popular that slot is, although you can also look out for monthly delivery-saver deals — but ultimately, it may work out to be less expensive to drive to the shop yourself. There's also a minimum amount that you must have in your basket to use this service. It's also worth noting that there is often difficulty with the availability of delivery slots, particularly around busy times of the year such as December or bank holidays.

With click and collect, you still have to book a slot, and the minimum spend of your basket still applies. However, there's usually a little more availability for collection slots, and you don't have to pay a fee for this service.

With both click and collect and delivery, you're also depending on the staff to pick products that are well within date and in good condition. You can also only use online payments for both services, so cash budgeters won't be able to use their physical envelopes to pay for the food shop. And of course, there are the substitutions – when something isn't in stock and a close alternative is packed for you instead. Sometimes these are a great deal – a premium version or a bigger packet for the same price – but other times the link to the original product can feel a little tenuous! Substitutions would drive me mad if they happened every week, and it makes it much harder to make a planned meal when something is swapped. Those living in the country may also have limited choices for these services – maybe fewer shops offer delivery or you have further to travel for click and collect.

On the plus side, both services can be great for busier lives and work well with budgeting. You can take your time and make sure you're getting everything on your list from the comfort of your own home. You can tick it off against your meal plan, and you can often amend your order too. You can also see the total and make sure you are not going over budget (without the potential stress of having to put things back at the till). There is also an online record of your previous orders, which can make the process quicker over time. It can also be handy to look back for inspiration – although I would recommend being careful not to just buy the same as the previous week every time. Stay intentional, even when shopping online.

What are the advantages of going into the shops, then? For me, a big one is that you can pick your own produce, choosing the one you most like the look of or the one with the latest sell-by date. You can also see the size of the products and it's easier to compare like for like if it's there in front of you.

Sometimes offers are only available in store, or even if they are valid online, it's often much easier to miss them – they can be much more visible in real life. You can also only purchase reduced-sticker items in store. And of course, you can use cash in the shop if you want to, so this method is a cash budgeter's friend. You likely won't accidentally buy the same groceries as last week; I certainly find it easier to be intentional when physically placing objects into my basket. You may end up purchasing less frequently, as when people have a delivery saver or a certain slot booked in advance, they usually feel they have to use it even if they don't need it. And by going into the store you are helping to support more local jobs; you also support local suppliers and smaller enterprises.

So, there are advantages and disadvantages to both ways of shopping, and ultimately it depends on you and which suits your household better. It may even depend on your current stage of life: I know that getting our shopping delivered the first couple of weeks after my babies were born was a lifesaver, but nowadays I do prefer to go into the store. It's important to weigh the pros and cons and decide which works best for you. It may be that you decide to try both for a trial period and then see which method saves you more money, but there is no right or wrong way to shop.

Side hustles

Side hustles, also known as nixers, odd jobs or side gigs, are opportunities for you to bring extra income into your budget. These can be one-off payments, or an income you receive more regularly. The extra income can then be used to reach your financial goals more quickly. Another major advantage is that an additional income source will make you less reliant on your main paycheque – so if your primary income is ever reduced or lost for any reason, you'll still have some money coming in. And we've all heard the stories of people who've been so successful in their side hustles that they've turned into their main source of income.

Whether that's your goal or not, what side hustles will work for you? Well, first, it's important to identify what spare time you have to undertake a side hustle. Almost all side hustles will require some time commitment, but some can be more involved than others. There's also cost: how much money will you need to carry out this side hustle? Do you need a qualification or skillset to get started? And are you living in an area where you can complete this side hustle?

The most successful side hustles usually evolve from an area that a person is already passionate about. In part, this can be due to the time commitment involved. If you have a hobby that you genuinely enjoy doing, it can be easier to continue committing to this in your spare time and then looking for a way to monetise it. Your hobby doesn't even need to be overly creative – if you're a self-confessed shopaholic, why not investigate becoming a mystery shopper for your local area? Doing online surveys, selling old clothes or homemade crafts; I could list other examples for days, but I honestly feel that a well-suited side hustle can be incredibly personal. For example, one teacher may be able to use their qualifications and extra time to give grinds, whereas another teacher may have family commitments that make the same set-up impossible.

There are three types of income that side hustles can provide you with.

Earned income

This is the most straightforward type, where you put in time and effort in exchange for income. A part-time job, for example, would fall into this category. You do the work and you get paid – simple.

Passive income

This type of income usually requires time, effort and often money to get up and running, but over time this income then starts to come in without any effort on your part. An example of a passive income would be renting a room in your house; you may have to spend time and money up front to prepare the room for rental, but then the income should come in regularly.

Capital-gains income

This applies to buying an item that increases in value over time, allowing you to then sell that item for a profit. Examples of this would be upcycling furniture or buying and selling stocks.

One thing that's important to remember about side hustles is that they are taxable. The great news, however, is this income is very easy to declare as long as it is under €5,000. There's a section on your income-tax return where you can declare additional income, at myAccount on revenue.ie. Anything over €5,000 must be submitted as a self-assessment on ROS; there is more information on this on revenue.ie. The only exception to this is any side hustle where you receive a voucher in return for your time – this is not taxable.

Hopefully this will have given you some ideas for side hustling. Try one out for a week or two – and remember, you're likely to find that some side hustles will work for you better than others. For example, I loved mystery shopping, but I would rarely get offered jobs that were less than half an hour from where I live, so it just wasn't worth it ... Nowadays, though, I love selling items we don't need from around the house!

No-spend days

A no-spend day is one during which you do not spend any money apart from on your bills, food or rent, etc. – basically, no unnecessary spending. Such days are a great tool for someone who struggles with impulsive spending. It doesn't mean that you have to cut out spending entirely, it just means that on certain days you are going consciously try and keep your unnecessary outgoings to zero.

Many people set a certain number of no-spend days as one of their goals each month. For example, they may aim to reach 16 no-spend days in the coming month; other people may try to have an entire no-spend month. This can be a great way of saving up for a large expense. It can also help when working on big goals like clearing debt, and it can be a good way of resetting your budget.

If you want to up the ante even further, you could also try a low-spend year. As I've already mentioned, my family had one in 2019. Just before the year started, we sat down with the kids and explained that this was a new journey that we would be starting for the year. For 365 days we would not be spending money, with only a few exceptions:

- We would still be paying rent, paying our bills, buying groceries and putting fuel in the car.

- We would still buy clothes and shoes, especially for the kids, but only to replace items that had worn out or that the kids had outgrown.
- We still bought gifts for friends and family. We did reduce our budget for these, but it was important to us that we were still able to celebrate with our loved ones.
- We could buy items if they were an investment, although we were very, very careful with this rule. For example, we saw a second-hand solid oak bed on an online marketplace for only €50, and decided that we were fine to buy it. It was a good deal – exactly the kind of furniture we were looking for – and we needed a bed.

In that low-spend year, we first cleared our credit-card debt – over €1,400 – in January. Then the aim was to save about €10,000 over the rest of the year, a goal of about €1,000 a month. This goal may seem big, but we had been renting for over 10 years at this stage, the rental market was worryingly low in availability and we really wanted to push towards saving our deposit.

So, our goal of saving over €1,000 per month was set and, being a little competitive, I really tried to beat that figure every month! Some months we managed to save a good bit more – one month we more than doubled our goal amount. In April, we were told that the house we were living in was going to be put on the market, and that we had until September to move out. Luckily, we were allowed to stay until then, because in June we had our offer on a house accepted. That year, we actually ended up saving over €15,000, and we got the keys for our own home at the very end of October! Without doing a low-spend year, becoming intentional with our spending and changing our habits, there's no way this would have been possible.

Now, the idea of a low-spend year can sound as though you'll be sitting at home, living a boring life … but this is where you get creative! We were adamant that our low-spend year would not become a low-fun year. We made plans every weekend, spent time with friends and family, went hiking around Ireland, had game nights and plenty of meals with friends. I even attended festivals that year – but I went for free by volunteering. We did more in 2019 than we had done in years, made more memories and spent more time with the people we loved. And thank goodness, because not only did we become very busy as homeowners and then with a third child, but of course the pandemic hit in 2020 and meant that we were all able to spend less time with friends and family. My point is that it's amazing how much fun can be had and how many memories made without spending money – but that can be easy to forget.

A low-spend year is not for everyone, but many people find a no-spend week or month very helpful, or even a target number of no-spend days, as I said before. Here are a couple of tips that may be useful for getting started:

- A week, month or year of minimal spending shouldn't be extended. Set your target amount of time, complete the period and then take a break.
- Inform family and friends that you are on a spending break, especially if it's for an extended period such as a month or a year. This makes turning down costly events easier, and they're likely to be much more open to your suggestions of free alternatives.
- Remember, you set the rules! What spending will you and will you not allow? You decide; this is your budget and your goal.
- It's important that your whole family is on board. Share the goal, share your *why*, and you will be much more likely to succeed.
- Set yourself up for success: choose a week or month to go no-spend that has fewer events and therefore less temptation.

Why not give it a go? The amount you save may surprise you ...

Part two

The year ahead

Now that we've been through the basics and covered some of the terminology around budgeting, it's time to look at the year ahead. What do you have coming up and, more importantly, where do you want to get to? Setting out clear goals is such an important step in committing to financial change.

Monthly goals

Write down the top two or three goals that you would like to achieve each month. This is your plan for the year ahead. What would you like to have achieved by this time next year? Plan that journey by setting manageable financial goals each month.

Month one:

Pay off holiday
Apply for UC.

Month two:

Save spending money for holiday

Month three:

Month four:

Monthly Goals

Month five:

___

Month six:

___

Month seven:

___

Month eight:

___

Month nine:

Month ten:

Month eleven:

Month twelve:

Let's get more specific with our goals!

Goal-setting is one of the best ways to clarify exactly what your financial aims are and how you are going to achieve them. They're also a great way of motivating you! Now, we've looked at your next year, but let's make the picture even bigger. I want you to think about where you want to be financially in six months', one year's and five years' time. What will your income look like? What will your savings balance be? As I said, we're getting specific here, so I want you to put down some numbers.

In six months ...

_____
_____
_____
_____

In one year ...

_____
_____
_____
_____

In five years ...

_____
_____
_____
_____

Where do you want to be five years from now?

The perfect day is a practice that I heard from a motivational speaker many years ago. My husband and I have completed this a few times, and it can be so interesting to look back on. You're going to describe your perfect day, five years from now: a day in your life when all of your financial goals have been met. I want you to describe your life, your home, your income. What do you work as? Who lives with you? Add as much detail as you can. As well as being something fun to look back on in the future, this exercise will motivate you and reveal which parts of your life are most important to you. The details you include here are your priorities; this exercise can remind you of what you need to focus on in order to achieve this perfect day.

Describe your perfect day.

Career goals and future plans

Reducing expenses will only help a budget so much. Ultimately, the quickest way to reach your financial goals is to increase your income. So, let's think about what you are — and can be — doing to achieve this. What total income would you like to bring in? Are you going to take up a side hustle, or increase the time you spend on one? Write your income goals for this year, next year and five years' time.

THIS YEAR:

\
\
\
\

NEXT YEAR:

\
\
\
\

IN FIVE YEARS:

\
\
\
\
\

Your vision board

This is a section for you to show your financial and lifestyle goals visually. It's up to you how you complete it — drawings, cut-outs, printouts and even words may help. I've included two pages in this section, so that if you have a partner there is room for you both to create separate boards if you prefer. This is a place to put images that motivate you, and we all have different motivators, so make these pages your own!

YOUR VISION BOARD

Memberships, subscriptions and large expenses

Now that you know where you want to *go*, it's time to take a look at where you *are* right now. We all have memberships and subscriptions that we've committed to and that we need to factor into our budgets. Looking at these in a list can be helpful because it may remind you that you no longer want or use certain things, and you may wish to cancel them. Maybe you signed up for a short-term membership deal, for example, but don't want to keep it going in the longer term. Keep coming back to this section throughout the year and add any new subscriptions that you commit to, as well as updating it if or when you cancel them!

List any of these types of expenses in the table on the next page. Don't forget larger ones that may be annual or infrequent, such as car insurance or tax, property tax or a six-month gym membership. Once you have listed these expenses, divide the yearly amount by 12 to give the monthly cost. You can set that amount aside each month to make your large expenses much more manageable.

MEMBERSHIPS, SUBSCRIPTIONS AND LARGE EXPENSES

Date	Details	Monthly amount	Yearly amount

What's coming up this year?

Even on a strict budget, it's important to be able to celebrate events that we want to throughout the year. Stay on top of this by listing below any events that are coming up this year that will impact your budget – for example, birthdays, weddings or holidays. You'll be able to see at a glance if you have a particularly busy time of year coming up and start saving accordingly (we'll look at how to map that out just over the page).

January	
February	
March	
April	
May	
June	
July	
August	
September	Holiday
October	
November	
December	Christmas

Saving your sinking funds

As I've already mentioned, it is important to save towards big expenses over time. Sinking funds are for those expenses we know are coming, usually with a due date and often a set amount, such as Christmas, birthdays, car maintenance or the kids going back to school. I recommend saving to a maximum of seven sinking funds at any one time.

Details	Total goal	Sinking fund	Date due

Savings tracker

So far, our focus has been on breaking things down to make your finances more manageable – but now it's time to take a look at the overall picture. This is a monthly balance tracker for all your different savings. Come back each month to fill in this table, making sure to include whether your various balances have increased or decreased each month.

Date	Emergency fund	Extra savings	Sinking funds	Total saved
Month one +/-				
Balance				
Month two +/-				
Balance				
Month three +/-				
Balance				
Month four +/-				
Balance				
Month five +/-				
Balance				

SAVINGS TRACKER

Date	Emergency fund	Extra savings	Sinking funds	Total saved
Month six +/-				
Balance				
Month seven +/-				
Balance				
Month eight +/-				
Balance				
Month nine +/-				
Balance				
Month ten +/-				
Balance				
Month eleven +/-				
Balance				
Month twelve +/-				
Balance				

Debts tracker

This section is where you're going to list your debts. If you made the minimum payment on a debt or borrowed more, put the amount you paid in the +/- monthly section. Next, if you made an extra payment on a debt, make a note of it here. Then make a note of your new balance for each debt. Remember, it's best to focus on overpaying only one debt at a time, using whichever method – either snowball or avalanche – you find most helpful.

List debts ⇨						Total paid
Month one +/-						
Extra paid						
Balance						
Month two +/-						
Extra paid						
Balance						
Month three +/-						
Extra paid						
Balance						
Month four +/-						
Extra paid						
Balance						
Month five +/-						
Extra paid						
Balance						

DEBTS TRACKER

List debts ⇨						Total paid
Month six +/-						
Extra paid						
Balance						
Month seven +/-						
Extra paid						
Balance						
Month eight +/-						
Extra paid						
Balance						
Month nine +/-						
Extra paid						
Balance						
Month ten +/-						
Extra paid						
Balance						
Month eleven +/-						
Extra paid						
Balance						
Month twelve +/-						
Extra paid						
Balance						

Bills and direct debits tracker

This next tracker will list all your bills and direct debts that are due every month. You'll need to refer to this section each month when making a note of these expenses on your calendar and in your budget. As each direct debit or fixed bill is paid, put a check mark in that month's column or colour in the little square!

Due date	Details	Amount due	Jan	Feb	Mar	Apr	May	Jun

BILLS AND DIRECT DEBITS TRACKER

Due date	Details	Amount due	Jul	Aug	Sep	Oct	Nov	Dec

Income tracker

Let's take a proper look at what's coming in! List your income details, income type and the total amount for each month. This is a great way of tracking side-hustle income, pay rises and bonus payments alongside your regular income.

Details	Income type	Jan	Feb	Mar

INCOME TRACKER

Apr	May	Jun	Jul	Aug	Sep	Oct	Nov	Dec	Total

Special occasions and gifts tracker

Here you are going to track special occasions and gifts to be given throughout the year. This includes occasions such as weddings, birthdays, christenings, holidays, even concerts – any time you might need to buy a present or spend money on a specific event. You will be saving for these occasions and events in your sinking funds, and this tracker will help you to make sure you are prepared and saving enough for the upcoming costs.

January

Event	Date	Amount	✓

February

Event	Date	Amount	✓

March

Event	Date	Amount	✓

April

Event	Date	Amount	✓

May

Event	Date	Amount	✓

June

Event	Date	Amount	✓

SPECIAL OCCASIONS AND GIFTS TRACKER

July

Event	Date	Amount	✓

August

Event	Date	Amount	✓

September

Event	Date	Amount	✓

October

Event	Date	Amount	✓

November

Event	Date	Amount	✓

December

Event	Date	Amount	✓

Part Three

How to track your spending

Beginning your budget

Now that you've decided on your financial goals and have a clear vision of what you would like to achieve – as well as an idea of future expenses that you'll need to prepare for – we are going to look at how you will start to plan your budget. I'll explain each section and provide examples of how I lay out my budget. I've put together worksheets and monthly calendars to help you work towards your goals, and by the end of this section you'll be ready to get started on your own budgeting journey!

Start by filling in the month at the front of your tracking section. It doesn't matter when you start this planner (so don't give yourself any excuses about waiting until the new year!); what matters is that you do start. The example budget I've filled in over the next couple of pages is for March.

This calendar is where you are going to mark down each paycheque and the bills and direct debits that need to come out of that paycheque. I like to highlight each paycheque in a different colour, and then use the same highlighter for all the bills that must be paid with that paycheque. That way, it's easy to see at a glance what has been paid and what is due with the next paycheque. Make sure that you also note down how much each bill or direct debit is for.

BEGINNING YOUR BUDGET

Your month at a glance

Mon	Tue	Wed	Thu	Fri	Sat	Sun
		1 Payday! Bank fees €9.00	2	3 Car insurance €42.15	4	5
6 Internet €52.20	7 Child benefit Mobile phone €19.99	8	9 Childcare €370.29	10	11 Gym membership €42.00	12
13	14	15 Payday!	16 Spotify €9.99	17 Credit card €178.16	18	19 Netflix €8.99
20 House insurance €38.41	21	22 Cable TV €39.00	23	24 Rent €850	25	26
27	28	29	30	31		

Key notes

Paycheque 1

Bills = €165.34

Child benefit

Bills = €370.29

Paycheque 2

Bills = €1,124.55

This month's goals

Remember those six-month, one-year and five-year goals you set earlier? Well, now it's time to break them down into more manageable goals for this month. Putting exact figures on these aims will help you to be clear about when you have achieved them. Remember to keep them realistic.

- ○ Save €200 into my emergency fund
- ○ Save €50 towards the kids going back to school
- ○ Cancel my cable TV subscription
- ○ Track my spending
- ○ _____
- ○ _____

How am I going to achieve them?

Once you have your goals set, note down how you're going to achieve them this month. What steps will you need to take? Will you need to change a habit, increase your income or reduce your spending? Make sure that you have a direct solution for each goal; this will help to keep the goals achievable.

- ○ Save €50 from each paycheque
- ○ Save €50 towards back-to-school from my first paycheque
- ○ Call and request a cancellation
- ○ Fill in my spending tracker every evening
- ○ _____
- ○ _____

BEGINNING YOUR BUDGET

Budget by paycheque

This is where you are going to create your budget – the plan for your finances over the next month. I've included space to make five budgets per month, so if you get paid weekly, fortnightly or monthly, you can make a plan for each paycheque. Some of you will need to use all five budget sheets, while others may be leaving some blank, depending on your pay frequency. You won't always need to use the date column – when budgeting for your everyday expenses in your cash envelopes, for example, allot an amount for the whole month – but you may decide you want to keep a record here of when things are due.

Paycheque name: _1 March paycheque - two weeks_

Income

Date	Details	Amount
1/3	1st March Paycheque	€1,150
	Side-hustle income	€60
Total		€1,210

Bills and direct debits

Date	Details	Amount
2/3	Banking fees	€9.00
3/3	Car insurance	€42.15
7/3	Mobile phone	€19.99
8/3	Internet	€52.20
13/3	Gym membership	€42.00
Total		€165.34

Cash or virtual envelopes

Date	Details	Amount
	Grocery shop	€300
	Petrol	€200
	Kids' treats	€30
	Meals out	€70
	Personal	€50
Total		€650

Debt pay-off

Date	Details	Amount
	Extra debt payment	€54.66
Total		€54.66

CAZ MOONEY'S BUDGETING PLANNER

Sinking funds

Date	Details	Amount
	Back to school	€50
	Gymnastics fees	€30
	Birthday fund	€30
	Holidays	€20
	Christmas	€10
Total		€140

Savings

Date	Details	Amount
	Emergency fund	€200
Total		€200

Summary

	Amount
Income	€1,210
Bills and direct debits	€165.34
Cash or virtual envelopes	€650
Sinking funds	€140
Debt	€54.66
Savings	€200

Income minus expenses = 0

Freezer inventory

This space is where you're going to keep a list of what is in your freezer at the start of the month. If you keep this section updated, you'll quickly be able to tell what you already have available for meals before creating your shopping list, and you'll be much less likely to waste food. It will also take you less time next month to complete this inventory once you're building off the list you already have!

So many food savings are made before you even go to the supermarket. By preparing this inventory thoroughly each month, you'll be able to create meals using ingredients you already have at home. I start with protein as a basis for my meals, so I have listed that first.

Protein		Vegetables	
Minced beef	○○●○○○	Broccoli	●○○○○○
Diced steak	○○○○○○	Garden peas	●○○○○○
Fish fingers	○○○○○○	Sweet peppers	●○○○○○
Vegan sausages	●○○○○○	Stir-fry veg	●○○○○○

Meals		Snacks and treats	
Chilli con carne	○○○○○○	Ice pops	●●●●○○
Pancakes	○●○○○○	Ice cream	●○○○○○
Breakfast waffles	○○○○○○	Cookies	●○○○○○

Miscellaneous			
Bread	○○●○○○	Bagels	●○○○○○
Butter	○○○○○○	Ice cubes	●○○○○○
Potato waffles	○○○○○○	Milk – whole	●○○○○○
Chicken stock	○○○○○○	Blueberries	●○○○○○
Vegetable stock	○○○○○○	Oven chips	●○○○○○

Meals I have at home

Once you have completed your freezer inventory, you'll probably have noticed ingredients that could form the basis for some meals in the month ahead. In this section you are going to list some meals that you could make over the next few weeks. Making one or two each week will help to reduce the cost of your food shop. First, write down the meal that you have in mind and the ingredients that you already have to make that meal. Then list the ingredients that you need to get (if any) to complete the meal.

Meal	Ingredients I already have		Ingredients I need
Spaghetti Bolognese	Minced beef Spaghetti Carrots	Spices Onions	Chopped tomatoes Mushrooms
Beef stew	Diced beef Carrots Parsnips	Onions Stock Broccoli	Potatoes
Chickpea curry	Chickpeas Rice Tomato purée	Onions Spices	Coconut milk Red pepper

Monthly meal planner

This section is for planning all your meals. I like to use this section weekly as I do my food shop weekly, but if you're a super-organised monthly shopper, you can plan out the full month ahead. You can plan just your main meal or breakfast, lunch and dinner – it's up to you. This section will then help you to make your shopping list. Prioritise ingredients that you already have, especially if they need to be eaten, and use the above section as well. I like to create meals using ingredients that are in season, on offer or reduced, and use supermarket apps, leaflets and websites to work out what these might be. If you use this section before you shop to plan your list and then stick to it, I'm sure you'll see great savings on your groceries.

CAZ MOONEY'S BUDGETING PLANNER

	Week one	Week two	Week three	Week four	Week five
Monday	Chicken, mushroom and rice bake	Leftover chicken pasta bake	Prawn stir-fry with noodles	Chilli con carne	Leftover beef and black beans with rice
Tuesday	Chilli con carne	Spag Bol	Creamy chicken pasta	Beef and bacon stew	Homemade burgers
Wednesday	Beef stew with mash	Chilli and garlic salmon	Sausage casserole	Hunter's chicken	Mushroom risotto
Thursday	Homemade burgers and wedges	Lentil stew	Lasagne and chips	Meatballs and spaghetti	Cottage pie
Friday	Chickpea curry with rice	Mac and cheese	Pesto bake	Turkey curry with rice	Paella
Saturday	Homemade pizzas	Sweet chilli chicken	Takeaway!	Chicken and corn bake	Chicken and leek pie
Sunday	Roast chicken	Pork chops and homemade chips	Fish pie	Roast beef	Family meal out!

Monthly spending tracker

Where does your money go? Just as you tracked your spending in preparation for writing your first budget, this is the space where you will now record your spending each month. Aim to fill this out every day so that you don't forget small costs, and then at the end of the month you can total each category to see how much you spent. You can use the highlighter colours that you previously assigned to each category to help you look back easily, and there is a section in your end-of-month recap to list your total spending in each category.

Date	Description	Category	Payment type	Amount
1/3	Doyle's s/s	Petrol	Cash	€50
	Kavanagh's supermarket	Food	Cash	€110
2/3	Parking	Personal	Cash	€3.00
	Bank fees	Bills and DDs	Direct debit	€9.00
3/3	Car insurance	Bills and DDs	Direct debit	€42.15
	Costa coffee	Eating out	Cash	€4.50
4/3	Maggie May's breakfast	Eating out	Cash	€42.35
6/3	Internet	Bills and DDs	Direct debit	€52.20
	Doyles s/s	Petrol	Cash	€70
7/3	Mobile phone	Bills and DDs	Direct debit	€19.99
	Kavanagh's supermarket	Food	Cash	€83.98
8/3	Katie's nail bar	Personal	Cash	€30

Monthly recap

This is an important section, as here you'll be able see exactly where your money went: how much income you received, how much you put towards your goals and how much you spent outside of that. These recaps are going to be the markers of your journey to your financial goals. By filling this out, you won't need to look back through multiple budgets, but will have your whole month in one place.

Income

Category	Income type	Amount
March paycheques 1, 2 and 3	Wages	€3,887
Side hustle	Additional income	€150
Child benefit	State payment	€420
	Total	€4,457

Spending

Category	Spending type	Amount
Food	Cash	€600
Petrol	Cash	€500
Personal	Cash	€100
Kids	Cash	€70
Bills and direct debits	Direct debits	€1,673.29
Sinking funds	Bank transfer	€800
Eating out	Cash	€80
Pets	Cash	€50
Miscellaneous	Cash	€72
Emergency fund	Bank transfer	€300
Extra debt	Bank transfer	€211.71
	Total	€4,457

In this table, list any debts that you're overpaying. Remember, I'd recommend that you focus only on overpaying on debt at a time, using your preferred method. The only time you might need to fill in more than one column here is if you've come to the end of one debt and have money left over to start throwing at your next debt – or if you have a larger-than-usual payment (say you got a bonus or tax rebate, for example) and are able to pay off multiple debts at once.

Extra debt payment					
List debt:	Credit card				
Current total:	€14,654				
Minimum payment:	€160				
Extra payment:	€211.71				
Total paid:	€371.71				Overall total paid
New balance:	€14,282.29				€371.71

CAZ MOONEY'S BUDGETING PLANNER

Here, note down any savings that you've made this month – for me, this is usually any contribution to my emergency fund and whatever sinking funds I'm working towards. You can keep track of the new balances in your funds, as well as the total figure that you've saved this month.

Savings and investments					
List savings/ investments:	Emergency fund	Summer holiday	Back-to-school	Jenny's birthday	
Paid in:	€300	€550	€175	€75	
New balance:	€450	€1,900	€350	€75	**Overall total paid**
Total paid:	€300	€550	€175	€75	€1,100

As your emergency fund is arguably the most important thing in your bank account, I also like to list its final balance separately at the end of the month – that way, I can see at a glance whether it's below €1,000 (if I've had to dip into it recently) and how much I'll need to top up to complete it again.

Emergency fund balance: _____ €450; €550 to go _____

Part Four

Let's get tracking

We've been through it all — now it's time for you to get started. Fill out each monthly section to make your own budget and keep track of how you're spending.

Month: JAN '24

"Your only limit is YOU"

CAZ MOONEY'S BUDGETING PLANNER

Your month at a glance

Use this calendar to record your paydays, along with the bills and direct debits that are due this month. I recommend using a highlighter to mark what needs to be paid from each paycheque in the same colour, and then you can record your totals in the key notes section. There's a full example of how I use this calendar on page 75.

Mon	Tue	Wed	Thu	Fri	Sat	Sun
1	2 ~~DD's~~ ~~£42~~	3	4	5	6	7
8	9	10 ~~DDS~~	11	12	13	14
15	16	17	18	19	20	21
22	23	24	~~25~~ PAY DAY	26	27	28
29	30	31				

Key notes

DD's £315

Standing order £335

BILL TOTAL £650

MONTH ONE

This month's goals

What goals are you hoping to achieve this month? Remember to set aims that will bring you closer to your six-month, one-year and five-year goals. To keep these goals achievable, make sure to write down the amount of money that you would like to save, pay off or earn. I have shared an example of how I lay out this section on page 76.

- PAY HOLIDAY £3200 in full ✓
- PAY MBNA in full
- Apply UC.
-
-
-

How am I going to achieve them?

Use this section to set out your plan to hit these goals. This will help you to keep them realistic.

-
-
-
-
-
-

CAZ MOONEY'S BUDGETING PLANNER

Budget by paycheque

This is your plan for your paycheque. By now, you should feel confident filling this out, and there's a mock budget on pages 77–8 that will walk you through step by step. Once you've filled in your income, expenses and financial goals, your income minus expenses should equal zero, as you're giving every cent a job.

Paycheque name: __JANUARY__

Income

Date	Details	Amount
5/1	CTC	150.94
9/1	CB	223.20
10/1	Nyree	40.00
12/1	CTC	150.94
15/1	SCP	200.00
17/1	reward	5.00
	refund	15.00
	Cheque	100.00
	Moved savings	3000.00
	" "	2313.54
	refund	20.00
	refund	50.00
	~~cheque~~ ebay	6.00
Total		

Cash or virtual envelopes

Date	Details	Amount
Total		

MONTH ONE

Bills and direct debits		
Date	Details	Amount
2/1	Aviva	8.54
2/1	BG services	19.91
10/1	EON	170.00
22/1	JD Gyms	19.99
27/1	Sky	20.98
29/1	Mobiles	23.00
2/1	TV lic.	13.25
8/1	Council tax	140.00
	Football	35.00
Total		

Debt pay-off N/A.		
Date	Details	Amount
Total		

CAZ MOONEY'S BUDGETING PLANNER

Sinking funds

Date	Details	Amount
Total		

Savings

Date	Details	Amount
	Lisa	150 —
	Fab	150 —
Total		

Summary

	Amount
Income	
Bills and direct debits	
Cash or virtual envelopes	
Sinking funds	
Debt	
Savings	

Income minus expenses = ____

MONTH ONE

Paycheque name: _____

Income		
Date	Details	Amount

Total

Cash or virtual envelopes		
Date	Details	Amount

Total

Bills and direct debits

Date	Details	Amount
Total		

Debt pay-off

Date	Details	Amount
Total		

MONTH ONE

Sinking funds

Date	Details	Amount
Total		

Savings

Date	Details	Amount
Total		

Summary

	Amount
Income	
Bills and direct debits	
Cash or virtual envelopes	
Sinking funds	
Debt	
Savings	

Income minus expenses = ____

Paycheque name: _____

Income		
Date	Details	Amount
Total		

Cash or virtual envelopes		
Date	Details	Amount
Total		

MONTH ONE

Bills and direct debits		
Date	Details	Amount
Total		

Debt pay-off		
Date	Details	Amount
Total		

CAZ MOONEY'S BUDGETING PLANNER

Sinking funds

Date	Details	Amount
Total		

Savings

Date	Details	Amount
Total		

Summary

	Amount
Income	
Bills and direct debits	
Cash or virtual envelopes	
Sinking funds	
Debt	
Savings	

Income minus expenses = ____

MONTH ONE

Paycheque name: _____

Income		
Date	Details	Amount
Total		

Cash or virtual envelopes		
Date	Details	Amount
Total		

Bills and direct debits

Date	Details	Amount
Total		

Debt pay-off

Date	Details	Amount
Total		

MONTH ONE

Sinking funds

Date	Details	Amount
Total		

Savings

Date	Details	Amount
Total		

Summary

	Amount
Income	
Bills and direct debits	
Cash or virtual envelopes	
Sinking funds	
Debt	
Savings	

Income minus expenses = ____

Paycheque name: _____

Income			
Date	Details		Amount

Total

Cash or virtual envelopes			
Date	Details		Amount

Total

MONTH ONE

Bills and direct debits		
Date	Details	Amount
Total		

Debt pay-off		
Date	Details	Amount
Total		

CAZ MOONEY'S BUDGETING PLANNER

Sinking funds

Date	Details	Amount
Total		

Savings

Date	Details	Amount
Total		

Summary

	Amount
Income	
Bills and direct debits	
Cash or virtual envelopes	
Sinking funds	
Debt	
Savings	

Income minus expenses = ____

MONTH ONE

Freezer inventory

At the start of every month, take a few minutes to complete a quick freezer inventory. This will help you to know exactly what you have at home, and you can use that information to create your meal plan, saving you time and money. See page 79 for an example of how this might look.

Protein		Vegetables	
	○○○○○○		○○○○○○
	○○○○○○		○○○○○○
	○○○○○○		○○○○○○
	○○○○○○		○○○○○○
	○○○○○○		○○○○○○
Meals		**Snacks and treats**	
	○○○○○○		○○○○○○
	○○○○○○		○○○○○○
	○○○○○○		○○○○○○
	○○○○○○		○○○○○○
	○○○○○○		○○○○○○
Miscellaneous			
	○○○○○○		○○○○○○
	○○○○○○		○○○○○○
	○○○○○○		○○○○○○
	○○○○○○		○○○○○○
	○○○○○○		○○○○○○

Meals I have at home

Making a note of meals that you already have at home will help reduce both food waste and the cost of your groceries. You may be short an ingredient or two for some meals, but the third column will make these easy to add to your shopping list. There's an example of this section on page 80.

Meal	Ingredients I already have	Ingredients I need

MONTH ONE

Monthly meal planner

Now it's time to plan your meals. This will help you to make efficient grocery lists and can be a great reminder to use up food that needs to be eaten. It's up to you whether you fill this section in weekly or monthly; there's an example of how I like to do it on page 82.

	Week one	Week two	Week three	Week four	Week five
Monday					
Tuesday					
Wednesday					
Thursday					
Friday					
Saturday					
Sunday					

Monthly spending tracker

Use this table to note where your money went this month. This will help you to reduce impulse spending and become more conscientious in how you spend your money. It's also very useful in helping you create your budget for the next month, as you can see where you need to allot your funds. See page 83 for a completed example of this tracker.

Date	Description	Category	Payment type	Amount

Monthly recap

It's time to look back over this month's finances. This section makes it easier to track your progress from month to month, and will help you to plan your financial goals for the next month. I've added an example of how I fill in this section on pages 84–6.

Income

Category	Income type	Amount
		Total

Spending

Category	Spending type	Amount
		Total

CAZ MOONEY'S BUDGETING PLANNER

Extra debt payment					
List debt					
Current total					
Minimum payment					
Extra payment					
Total paid					**Overall total paid**
New balance					

Savings and investments					
List savings/investments					
Paid in					
New balance					**Overall total paid**
Total paid					

Emergency fund balance: _____

MONTH ONE

Monthly wins

Use this calendar to record the things you've done right this month – whether that's cancelling a subscription that you no longer need, clearing a debt or starting an extra side hustle. I also like to use it to track my no-spend days – so any day that I don't spend anything on non-essentials, I'll colour in or sometimes mark with a little sticker star. Remember, every win, no matter how small, is bringing you one step closer to your goals!

Mon	Tue	Wed	Thu	Fri	Sat	Sun

Month: _____

" **Small wins become big wins** "

MONTH TWO

Your month at a glance

Use this calendar to record your paydays, along with the bills and direct debits that are due this month. I recommend using a highlighter to mark what needs to be paid from each paycheque in the same colour, and then you can record your totals in the key notes section. There's a full example of how I use this calendar on page 75.

Mon	Tue	Wed	Thu	Fri	Sat	Sun

Key notes

_____

_____

_____

This month's goals

What goals are you hoping to achieve this month? Remember to set aims that will bring you closer to your six-month, one-year and five-year goals. To keep these goals achievable, make sure to write down the amount of money that you would like to save, pay off or earn. I have shared an example of how I lay out this section on page 76.

- _____
- _____
- _____
- _____
- _____
- _____

How am I going to achieve them?

Use this section to set out your plan to hit these goals. This will help you to keep them realistic.

- _____
- _____
- _____
- _____
- _____
- _____

MONTH TWO

Budget by paycheque

This is your plan for your paycheque. By now, you should feel confident filling this out, and there's a mock budget on pages 77–8 that will walk you through step by step. Once you've filled in your income, expenses and financial goals, your income minus expenses should equal zero, as you're giving every cent a job.

Paycheque name: _____

Income		
Date	Details	Amount
Total		

Cash or virtual envelopes		
Date	Details	Amount
Total		

Bills and direct debits

Date	Details	Amount
Total		

Debt pay-off

Date	Details	Amount
Total		

MONTH TWO

Sinking funds

Date	Details	Amount
Total		

Savings

Date	Details	Amount
Total		

Summary

	Amount
Income	
Bills and direct debits	
Cash or virtual envelopes	
Sinking funds	
Debt	
Savings	

Income minus expenses = ____

Paycheque name: _____

Income		
Date	Details	Amount
Total		

Cash or virtual envelopes		
Date	Details	Amount
Total		

MONTH TWO

Bills and direct debits				Debt pay-off		
Date	Details	Amount	Date	Details	Amount
Total			Total		

Sinking funds

Date	Details	Amount
Total		

Savings

Date	Details	Amount
Total		

Summary

	Amount
Income	
Bills and direct debits	
Cash or virtual envelopes	
Sinking funds	
Debt	
Savings	

Income minus expenses = ____

MONTH TWO

Paycheque name: _____

Income		
Date	Details	Amount
Total		

Cash or virtual envelopes		
Date	Details	Amount
Total		

Bills and direct debits

Date	Details	Amount
Total		

Debt pay-off

Date	Details	Amount
Total		

MONTH TWO

Sinking funds

Date	Details	Amount

Total

Savings

Date	Details	Amount

Total

Summary

	Amount
Income	
Bills and direct debits	
Cash or virtual envelopes	
Sinking funds	
Debt	
Savings	

Income minus expenses = ____

Paycheque name: _____

Income		
Date	Details	Amount
Total		

Cash or virtual envelopes		
Date	Details	Amount
Total		

MONTH TWO

Bills and direct debits		
Date	Details	Amount

Total

Debt pay-off		
Date	Details	Amount

Total

Sinking funds

Date	Details	Amount

Total

Savings

Date	Details	Amount

Total

Summary

	Amount
Income	
Bills and direct debits	
Cash or virtual envelopes	
Sinking funds	
Debt	
Savings	

Income minus expenses = ____

MONTH TWO

Paycheque name: _____

Income		
Date	Details	Amount

Total

Cash or virtual envelopes		
Date	Details	Amount

Total

Bills and direct debits

Date	Details	Amount
Total		

Debt pay-off

Date	Details	Amount
Total		

MONTH TWO

Sinking funds

Date	Details	Amount
Total		

Savings

Date	Details	Amount
Total		

Summary

	Amount
Income	
Bills and direct debits	
Cash or virtual envelopes	
Sinking funds	
Debt	
Savings	

Income minus expenses = ____

Freezer inventory

At the start of every month, take a few minutes to complete a quick freezer inventory. This will help you to know exactly what you have at home, and you can use that information to create your meal plan, saving you time and money. See page 79 for an example of how this might look.

Protein		Vegetables	
	○○○○○○		○○○○○○
	○○○○○○		○○○○○○
	○○○○○○		○○○○○○
	○○○○○○		○○○○○○
	○○○○○○		○○○○○○

Meals		Snacks and treats	
	○○○○○○		○○○○○○
	○○○○○○		○○○○○○
	○○○○○○		○○○○○○
	○○○○○○		○○○○○○
	○○○○○○		○○○○○○

Miscellaneous			
	○○○○○○		○○○○○○
	○○○○○○		○○○○○○
	○○○○○○		○○○○○○
	○○○○○○		○○○○○○
	○○○○○○		○○○○○○

MONTH TWO

Meals I have at home

Making a note of meals that you already have at home will help reduce both food waste and the cost of your groceries. You may be short an ingredient or two for some meals, but the third column will make these easy to add to your shopping list. There's an example of this section on page 80.

Meal	Ingredients I already have	Ingredients I need

Monthly meal planner

Now it's time to plan your meals. This will help you to make efficient grocery lists and can be a great reminder to use up food that needs to be eaten. It's up to you whether you fill this section in weekly or monthly; there's an example of how I like to do it on page 82.

	Week one	Week two	Week three	Week four	Week five
Monday					
Tuesday					
Wednesday					
Thursday					
Friday					
Saturday					
Sunday					

MONTH TWO

Monthly spending tracker

Use this table to note where your money went this month. This will help you to reduce impulse spending and become more conscientious in how you spend your money. It's also very useful in helping you create your budget for the next month, as you can see where you need to allot your funds. See page 83 for a completed example of this tracker.

Date	Description	Category	Payment type	Amount

Monthly recap

It's time to look back over this month's finances. This section makes it easier to track your progress from month to month, and will help you to plan your financial goals for the next month. I've added an example of how I fill in this section on pages 84–6.

Income		
Category	Income type	Amount
	Total	

Spending		
Category	Spending type	Amount
	Total	

MONTH TWO

Extra debt payment					
List debt					
Current total					
Minimum payment					
Extra payment					
Total paid					**Overall total paid**
New balance					

Savings and investments					
List savings/investments					
Paid in					
New balance					**Overall total paid**
Total paid					

Emergency fund balance: _____

Monthly wins

Use this calendar to record the things you've done right this month – whether that's cancelling a subscription that you no longer need, clearing a debt or starting an extra side hustle. I also like to use it to track my no-spend days – so any day that I don't spend anything on non-essentials, I'll colour in or sometimes mark with a little sticker star. Remember, every win, no matter how small, is bringing you one step closer to your goals!

Mon	Tue	Wed	Thu	Fri	Sat	Sun

Month: _____

> "Don't go broke trying to follow others"

Your month at a glance

Use this calendar to record your paydays, along with the bills and direct debits that are due this month. I recommend using a highlighter to mark what needs to be paid from each paycheque in the same colour, and then you can record your totals in the key notes section. There's a full example of how I use this calendar on page 75.

Mon	Tue	Wed	Thu	Fri	Sat	Sun

Key notes

_____

_____

_____

_____

MONTH THREE

This month's goals

What goals are you hoping to achieve this month? Remember to set aims that will bring you closer to your six-month, one-year and five-year goals. To keep these goals achievable, make sure to write down the amount of money that you would like to save, pay off or earn. I have shared an example of how I lay out this section on page 76.

○ _____

○ _____

○ _____

○ _____

○ _____

○ _____

How am I going to achieve them?

Use this section to set out your plan to hit these goals. This will help you to keep them realistic.

○ _____

○ _____

○ _____

○ _____

○ _____

○ _____

Budget by paycheque

This is your plan for your paycheque. By now, you should feel confident filling this out, and there's a mock budget on pages 77–8 that will walk you through step by step. Once you've filled in your income, expenses and financial goals, your income minus expenses should equal zero, as you're giving every cent a job.

Paycheque name: _____

Income		
Date	Details	Amount
Total		

Cash or virtual envelopes		
Date	Details	Amount
Total		

MONTH THREE

Bills and direct debits		
Date	Details	Amount
Total		

Debt pay-off		
Date	Details	Amount
Total		

CAZ MOONEY'S BUDGETING PLANNER

Sinking funds

Date	Details	Amount
Total		

Savings

Date	Details	Amount
Total		

Summary

	Amount
Income	
Bills and direct debits	
Cash or virtual envelopes	
Sinking funds	
Debt	
Savings	

Income minus expenses = ____

MONTH THREE

Paycheque name: _____

Income		
Date	Details	Amount

Total

Cash or virtual envelopes		
Date	Details	Amount

Total

CAZ MOONEY'S BUDGETING PLANNER

Bills and direct debits		
Date	Details	Amount
Total		

Debt pay-off		
Date	Details	Amount
Total		

MONTH THREE

Sinking funds

Date	Details	Amount
Total		

Savings

Date	Details	Amount
Total		

Summary

	Amount
Income	
Bills and direct debits	
Cash or virtual envelopes	
Sinking funds	
Debt	
Savings	

Income minus expenses = _____

CAZ MOONEY'S BUDGETING PLANNER

Paycheque name: _____

Income		
Date	Details	Amount
Total		

Cash or virtual envelopes		
Date	Details	Amount
Total		

MONTH THREE

Bills and direct debits		
Date	Details	Amount

Total

Debt pay-off		
Date	Details	Amount

Total

CAZ MOONEY'S BUDGETING PLANNER

Sinking funds

Date	Details	Amount
Total		

Savings

Date	Details	Amount
Total		

Summary

	Amount
Income	
Bills and direct debits	
Cash or virtual envelopes	
Sinking funds	
Debt	
Savings	

Income minus expenses = ____

Paycheque name: _____

Income		
Date	Details	Amount
Total		

Cash or virtual envelopes		
Date	Details	Amount
Total		

CAZ MOONEY'S BUDGETING PLANNER

Bills and direct debits		
Date	Details	Amount
Total		

Debt pay-off		
Date	Details	Amount
Total		

MONTH THREE

Sinking funds

Date	Details	Amount

Total

Savings

Date	Details	Amount

Total

Summary

	Amount
Income	
Bills and direct debits	
Cash or virtual envelopes	
Sinking funds	
Debt	
Savings	

Income minus expenses = ____

Paycheque name: _____

Income		
Date	Details	Amount
Total		

Cash or virtual envelopes		
Date	Details	Amount
Total		

MONTH THREE

Bills and direct debits		
Date	Details	Amount
Total		

Debt pay-off		
Date	Details	Amount
Total		

CAZ MOONEY'S BUDGETING PLANNER

Sinking funds

Date	Details	Amount
Total		

Savings

Date	Details	Amount
Total		

Summary

	Amount
Income	
Bills and direct debits	
Cash or virtual envelopes	
Sinking funds	
Debt	
Savings	

Income minus expenses = ____

MONTH THREE

Freezer inventory

At the start of every month, take a few minutes to complete a quick freezer inventory. This will help you to know exactly what you have at home, and you can use that information to create your meal plan, saving you time and money. See page 79 for an example of how this might look.

Protein		Vegetables	
	○○○○○○		○○○○○○
	○○○○○○		○○○○○○
	○○○○○○		○○○○○○
	○○○○○○		○○○○○○
	○○○○○○		○○○○○○

Meals		Snacks and treats	
	○○○○○○		○○○○○○
	○○○○○○		○○○○○○
	○○○○○○		○○○○○○
	○○○○○○		○○○○○○
	○○○○○○		○○○○○○

Miscellaneous			
	○○○○○○		○○○○○○
	○○○○○○		○○○○○○
	○○○○○○		○○○○○○
	○○○○○○		○○○○○○
	○○○○○○		○○○○○○

Meals I have at home

Making a note of meals that you already have at home will help reduce both food waste and the cost of your groceries. You may be short an ingredient or two for some meals, but the third column will make these easy to add to your shopping list. There's an example of this section on page 80.

Meal	Ingredients I already have	Ingredients I need

MONTH THREE

Monthly meal planner

Now it's time to plan your meals. This will help you to make efficient grocery lists and can be a great reminder to use up food that needs to be eaten. It's up to you whether you fill this section in weekly or monthly; there's an example of how I like to do it on page 82.

	Week one	Week two	Week three	Week four	Week five
Monday					
Tuesday					
Wednesday					
Thursday					
Friday					
Saturday					
Sunday					

Monthly spending tracker

Use this table to note where your money went this month. This will help you to reduce impulse spending and become more conscientious in how you spend your money. It's also very useful in helping you create your budget for the next month, as you can see where you need to allot your funds. See page 83 for a completed example of this tracker.

Date	Description	Category	Payment type	Amount

Monthly recap

It's time to look back over this month's finances. This section makes it easier to track your progress from month to month, and will help you to plan your financial goals for the next month. I've added an example of how I fill in this section on pages 84–6.

Income		
Category	Income type	Amount
	Total	

Spending		
Category	Spending type	Amount
	Total	

CAZ MOONEY'S BUDGETING PLANNER

Extra debt payment

List debt					
Current total					
Minimum payment					
Extra payment					
Total paid					**Overall total paid**
New balance					

Savings and investments

List savings/ investments					
Paid in					
New balance					**Overall total paid**
Total paid					

Emergency fund balance: _____

MONTH THREE

Monthly wins

Use this calendar to record the things you've done right this month – whether that's cancelling a subscription that you no longer need, clearing a debt or starting an extra side hustle. I also like to use it to track my no-spend days – so any day that I don't spend anything on non-essentials, I'll colour in or sometimes mark with a little sticker star. Remember, every win, no matter how small, is bringing you one step closer to your goals!

Mon	Tue	Wed	Thu	Fri	Sat	Sun

Month: _____

> "Every cent towards that goal counts!"

MONTH FOUR

Your month at a glance

Use this calendar to record your paydays, along with the bills and direct debits that are due this month. I recommend using a highlighter to mark what needs to be paid from each paycheque in the same colour, and then you can record your totals in the key notes section. There's a full example of how I use this calendar on page 75.

Mon	Tue	Wed	Thu	Fri	Sat	Sun

Key notes
_____
_____
_____

This month's goals

What goals are you hoping to achieve this month? Remember to set aims that will bring you closer to your six-month, one-year and five-year goals. To keep these goals achievable, make sure to write down the amount of money that you would like to save, pay off or earn. I have shared an example of how I lay out this section on page 76.

- _____
- _____
- _____
- _____
- _____
- _____

How am I going to achieve them?

Use this section to set out your plan to hit these goals. This will help you to keep them realistic.

- _____
- _____
- _____
- _____
- _____
- _____

MONTH FOUR

Budget by paycheque

This is your plan for your paycheque. By now, you should feel confident filling this out, and there's a mock budget on pages 77–8 that will walk you through step by step. Once you've filled in your income, expenses and financial goals, your income minus expenses should equal zero, as you're giving every cent a job.

Paycheque name: _____

Income		
Date	Details	Amount
Total		

Cash or virtual envelopes		
Date	Details	Amount
Total		

Bills and direct debits

Date	Details	Amount
Total		

Debt pay-off

Date	Details	Amount
Total		

MONTH FOUR

Sinking funds

Date	Details	Amount
Total		

Savings

Date	Details	Amount
Total		

Summary

	Amount
Income	
Bills and direct debits	
Cash or virtual envelopes	
Sinking funds	
Debt	
Savings	

Income minus expenses = ____

CAZ MOONEY'S BUDGETING PLANNER

Paycheque name: _____

Income		
Date	Details	Amount
Total		

Cash or virtual envelopes		
Date	Details	Amount
Total		

MONTH FOUR

Bills and direct debits				Debt pay-off			
Date	Details		Amount	Date	Details		Amount

Total | | | | Total | | |

CAZ MOONEY'S BUDGETING PLANNER

Sinking funds

Date	Details	Amount
Total		

Savings

Date	Details	Amount
Total		

Summary

	Amount
Income	
Bills and direct debits	
Cash or virtual envelopes	
Sinking funds	
Debt	
Savings	

Income minus expenses = ____

MONTH FOUR

Paycheque name: _____

Income		
Date	Details	Amount
Total		

Cash or virtual envelopes		
Date	Details	Amount
Total		

CAZ MOONEY'S BUDGETING PLANNER

Bills and direct debits

Date	Details	Amount
Total		

Debt pay-off

Date	Details	Amount
Total		

MONTH FOUR

Sinking funds

Date	Details	Amount

Total

Savings

Date	Details	Amount

Total

Summary

	Amount
Income	
Bills and direct debits	
Cash or virtual envelopes	
Sinking funds	
Debt	
Savings	

Income minus expenses = ____

CAZ MOONEY'S BUDGETING PLANNER

Paycheque name: _____

Income		
Date	Details	Amount
Total		

Cash or virtual envelopes		
Date	Details	Amount
Total		

MONTH FOUR

Bills and direct debits

Date	Details	Amount

Total

Debt pay-off

Date	Details	Amount

Total

CAZ MOONEY'S BUDGETING PLANNER

Sinking funds

Date	Details	Amount
Total		

Savings

Date	Details	Amount
Total		

Summary

	Amount
Income	
Bills and direct debits	
Cash or virtual envelopes	
Sinking funds	
Debt	
Savings	

Income minus expenses = ____

MONTH FOUR

Paycheque name: _____

Income		
Date	Details	Amount

Total

Cash or virtual envelopes		
Date	Details	Amount

Total

CAZ MOONEY'S BUDGETING PLANNER

Bills and direct debits		
Date	Details	Amount
Total		

Debt pay-off		
Date	Details	Amount
Total		

MONTH FOUR

Sinking funds

Date	Details	Amount

Total

Savings

Date	Details	Amount

Total

Summary

	Amount
Income	
Bills and direct debits	
Cash or virtual envelopes	
Sinking funds	
Debt	
Savings	

Income minus expenses = ____

Freezer inventory

At the start of every month, take a few minutes to complete a quick freezer inventory. This will help you to know exactly what you have at home, and you can use that information to create your meal plan, saving you time and money. See page 79 for an example of how this might look.

Protein		Vegetables	
	○○○○○○		○○○○○○
	○○○○○○		○○○○○○
	○○○○○○		○○○○○○
	○○○○○○		○○○○○○
	○○○○○○		○○○○○○
Meals		Snacks and treats	
	○○○○○○		○○○○○○
	○○○○○○		○○○○○○
	○○○○○○		○○○○○○
	○○○○○○		○○○○○○
	○○○○○○		○○○○○○
Miscellaneous			
	○○○○○○		○○○○○○
	○○○○○○		○○○○○○
	○○○○○○		○○○○○○
	○○○○○○		○○○○○○
	○○○○○○		○○○○○○

MONTH FOUR

Meals I have at home

Making a note of meals that you already have at home will help reduce both food waste and the cost of your groceries. You may be short an ingredient or two for some meals, but the third column will make these easy to add to your shopping list. There's an example of this section on page 80.

Meal	Ingredients I already have	Ingredients I need

Monthly meal planner

Now it's time to plan your meals. This will help you to make efficient grocery lists and can be a great reminder to use up food that needs to be eaten. It's up to you whether you fill this section in weekly or monthly; there's an example of how I like to do it on page 82.

	Week one	Week two	Week three	Week four	Week five
Monday					
Tuesday					
Wednesday					
Thursday					
Friday					
Saturday					
Sunday					

MONTH FOUR

Monthly spending tracker

Use this table to note where your money went this month. This will help you to reduce impulse spending and become more conscientious in how you spend your money. It's also very useful in helping you create your budget for the next month, as you can see where you need to allot your funds. See page 83 for a completed example of this tracker.

Date	Description	Category	Payment type	Amount

Monthly recap

It's time to look back over this month's finances. This section makes it easier to track your progress from month to month, and will help you to plan your financial goals for the next month. I've added an example of how I fill in this section on pages 84–6.

Income		
Category	Income type	Amount
	Total	

Spending		
Category	Spending type	Amount
	Total	

MONTH FOUR

Extra debt payment

List debt					
Current total					
Minimum payment					
Extra payment					
Total paid					**Overall total paid**
New balance					

Savings and investments

List savings/investments					
Paid in					
New balance					**Overall total paid**
Total paid					

Emergency fund balance: _____

Monthly wins

Use this calendar to record the things you've done right this month – whether that's cancelling a subscription that you no longer need, clearing a debt or starting an extra side hustle. I also like to use it to track my no-spend days – so any day that I don't spend anything on non-essentials, I'll colour in or sometimes mark with a little sticker star. Remember, every win, no matter how small, is bringing you one step closer to your goals!

Mon	Tue	Wed	Thu	Fri	Sat	Sun

Month: _____

> **"If it's not in the budget, it's okay to say no"**

Your month at a glance

Use this calendar to record your paydays, along with the bills and direct debits that are due this month. I recommend using a highlighter to mark what needs to be paid from each paycheque in the same colour, and then you can record your totals in the key notes section. There's a full example of how I use this calendar on page 75.

Mon	Tue	Wed	Thu	Fri	Sat	Sun

Key notes

_____
_____
_____

MONTH FIVE

This month's goals

What goals are you hoping to achieve this month? Remember to set aims that will bring you closer to your six-month, one-year and five-year goals. To keep these goals achievable, make sure to write down the amount of money that you would like to save, pay off or earn. I have shared an example of how I lay out this section on page 76.

○ _____

○ _____

○ _____

○ _____

○ _____

○ _____

How am I going to achieve them?

Use this section to set out your plan to hit these goals. This will help you to keep them realistic.

○ _____

○ _____

○ _____

○ _____

○ _____

○ _____

Budget by paycheque

This is your plan for your paycheque. By now, you should feel confident filling this out, and there's a mock budget on pages 77–8 that will walk you through step by step. Once you've filled in your income, expenses and financial goals, your income minus expenses should equal zero, as you're giving every cent a job.

Paycheque name: _____

Income		
Date	Details	Amount
Total		

Cash or virtual envelopes		
Date	Details	Amount
Total		

MONTH FIVE

Bills and direct debits		
Date	Details	Amount
Total		

Debt pay-off		
Date	Details	Amount
Total		

CAZ MOONEY'S BUDGETING PLANNER

Sinking funds

Date	Details	Amount
Total		

Savings

Date	Details	Amount
Total		

Summary

	Amount
Income	
Bills and direct debits	
Cash or virtual envelopes	
Sinking funds	
Debt	
Savings	

Income minus expenses = ____

MONTH FIVE

Paycheque name: _____

Income		
Date	Details	Amount

Total

Cash or virtual envelopes		
Date	Details	Amount

Total

CAZ MOONEY'S BUDGETING PLANNER

Bills and direct debits

Date	Details	Amount
Total		

Debt pay-off

Date	Details	Amount
Total		

MONTH FIVE

Sinking funds

Date	Details	Amount

Total

Savings

Date	Details	Amount

Total

Summary

	Amount
Income	
Bills and direct debits	
Cash or virtual envelopes	
Sinking funds	
Debt	
Savings	

Income minus expenses = ____

CAZ MOONEY'S BUDGETING PLANNER

Paycheque name: _____

Income		
Date	Details	Amount
Total		

Cash or virtual envelopes		
Date	Details	Amount
Total		

MONTH FIVE

Bills and direct debits		
Date	Details	Amount
Total		

Debt pay-off		
Date	Details	Amount
Total		

CAZ MOONEY'S BUDGETING PLANNER

Sinking funds

Date	Details	Amount
Total		

Savings

Date	Details	Amount
Total		

Summary

	Amount
Income	
Bills and direct debits	
Cash or virtual envelopes	
Sinking funds	
Debt	
Savings	

Income minus expenses = ____

MONTH FIVE

Paycheque name: _____

Income			
Date	Details		Amount
Total			

Cash or virtual envelopes			
Date	Details		Amount
Total			

CAZ MOONEY'S BUDGETING PLANNER

Bills and direct debits				Debt pay-off			
Date	Details		Amount	Date	Details		Amount
Total				Total			

MONTH FIVE

Sinking funds

Date	Details	Amount

Total

Savings

Date	Details	Amount

Total

Summary

	Amount
Income	
Bills and direct debits	
Cash or virtual envelopes	
Sinking funds	
Debt	
Savings	

Income minus expenses = ____

CAZ MOONEY'S BUDGETING PLANNER

Paycheque name: _____

Income		
Date	Details	Amount
Total		

Cash or virtual envelopes		
Date	Details	Amount
Total		

MONTH FIVE

Bills and direct debits

Date	Details	Amount

Total

Debt pay-off

Date	Details	Amount

Total

CAZ MOONEY'S BUDGETING PLANNER

Sinking funds

Date	Details	Amount
Total		

Savings

Date	Details	Amount
Total		

Summary

	Amount
Income	
Bills and direct debits	
Cash or virtual envelopes	
Sinking funds	
Debt	
Savings	

Income minus expenses = ____

Freezer inventory

At the start of every month, take a few minutes to complete a quick freezer inventory. This will help you to know exactly what you have at home, and you can use that information to create your meal plan, saving you time and money. See page 79 for an example of how this might look.

Protein		Vegetables	
	○○○○○○		○○○○○○
	○○○○○○		○○○○○○
	○○○○○○		○○○○○○
	○○○○○○		○○○○○○
	○○○○○○		○○○○○○

Meals		Snacks and treats	
	○○○○○○		○○○○○○
	○○○○○○		○○○○○○
	○○○○○○		○○○○○○
	○○○○○○		○○○○○○
	○○○○○○		○○○○○○

Miscellaneous			
	○○○○○○		○○○○○○
	○○○○○○		○○○○○○
	○○○○○○		○○○○○○
	○○○○○○		○○○○○○
	○○○○○○		○○○○○○

Meals I have at home

Making a note of meals that you already have at home will help reduce both food waste and the cost of your groceries. You may be short an ingredient or two for some meals, but the third column will make these easy to add to your shopping list. There's an example of this section on page 80.

Meal	Ingredients I already have	Ingredients I need

Monthly meal planner

Now it's time to plan your meals. This will help you to make efficient grocery lists and can be a great reminder to use up food that needs to be eaten. It's up to you whether you fill this section in weekly or monthly; there's an example of how I like to do it on page 82.

	Week one	Week two	Week three	Week four	Week five
Monday					
Tuesday					
Wednesday					
Thursday					
Friday					
Saturday					
Sunday					

Monthly spending tracker

Use this table to note where your money went this month. This will help you to reduce impulse spending and become more conscientious in how you spend your money. It's also very useful in helping you create your budget for the next month, as you can see where you need to allot your funds. See page 83 for a completed example of this tracker.

Date	Description	Category	Payment type	Amount

MONTH FIVE

Monthly recap

It's time to look back over this month's finances. This section makes it easier to track your progress from month to month, and will help you to plan your financial goals for the next month. I've added an example of how I fill in this section on pages 84–6.

Income		
Category	Income type	Amount
	Total	

Spending		
Category	Spending type	Amount
	Total	

CAZ MOONEY'S BUDGETING PLANNER

Extra debt payment

List debt					
Current total					
Minimum payment					
Extra payment					
Total paid					**Overall total paid**
New balance					

Savings and investments

List savings/investments					
Paid in					
New balance					**Overall total paid**
Total paid					

Emergency fund balance: _____

MONTH FIVE

Monthly wins

Use this calendar to record the things you've done right this month — whether that's cancelling a subscription that you no longer need, clearing a debt or starting an extra side hustle. I also like to use it to track my no-spend days — so any day that I don't spend anything on non-essentials, I'll colour in or sometimes mark with a little sticker star. Remember, every win, no matter how small, is bringing you one step closer to your goals!

Mon	Tue	Wed	Thu	Fri	Sat	Sun

Month: _____

> " **Take control of your money so that it doesn't control you** "

MONTH SIX

Your month at a glance

Use this calendar to record your paydays, along with the bills and direct debits that are due this month. I recommend using a highlighter to mark what needs to be paid from each paycheque in the same colour, and then you can record your totals in the key notes section. There's a full example of how I use this calendar on page 75.

Mon	Tue	Wed	Thu	Fri	Sat	Sun

Key notes
_____
_____
_____
_____

This month's goals

What goals are you hoping to achieve this month? Remember to set aims that will bring you closer to your six-month, one-year and five-year goals. To keep these goals achievable, make sure to write down the amount of money that you would like to save, pay off or earn. I have shared an example of how I lay out this section on page 76.

○ _____

○ _____

○ _____

○ _____

○ _____

○ _____

How am I going to achieve them?

Use this section to set out your plan to hit these goals. This will help you to keep them realistic.

○ _____

○ _____

○ _____

○ _____

○ _____

○ _____

MONTH SIX

Budget by paycheque

This is your plan for your paycheque. By now, you should feel confident filling this out, and there's a mock budget on pages 77–8 that will walk you through step by step. Once you've filled in your income, expenses and financial goals, your income minus expenses should equal zero, as you're giving every cent a job.

Paycheque name: _____

Income		
Date	Details	Amount
Total		

Cash or virtual envelopes		
Date	Details	Amount
Total		

CAZ MOONEY'S BUDGETING PLANNER

Bills and direct debits		
Date	Details	Amount
Total		

Debt pay-off		
Date	Details	Amount
Total		

MONTH SIX

Sinking funds

Date	Details	Amount

Total

Savings

Date	Details	Amount

Total

Summary

	Amount
Income	
Bills and direct debits	
Cash or virtual envelopes	
Sinking funds	
Debt	
Savings	

Income minus expenses = ____

Paycheque name: _____

Income		
Date	Details	Amount
Total		

Cash or virtual envelopes		
Date	Details	Amount
Total		

MONTH SIX

Bills and direct debits		
Date	Details	Amount
Total		

Debt pay-off		
Date	Details	Amount
Total		

CAZ MOONEY'S BUDGETING PLANNER

Sinking funds

Date	Details	Amount
Total		

Savings

Date	Details	Amount
Total		

Summary

	Amount
Income	
Bills and direct debits	
Cash or virtual envelopes	
Sinking funds	
Debt	
Savings	

Income minus expenses = ____

MONTH SIX

Paycheque name: _____

Income				Cash or virtual envelopes			
Date	Details		Amount	Date	Details		Amount
Total				Total			

CAZ MOONEY'S BUDGETING PLANNER

Bills and direct debits		
Date	Details	Amount
Total		

Debt pay-off		
Date	Details	Amount
Total		

MONTH SIX

Sinking funds

Date	Details	Amount
Total		

Savings

Date	Details	Amount
Total		

Summary

	Amount
Income	
Bills and direct debits	
Cash or virtual envelopes	
Sinking funds	
Debt	
Savings	

Income minus expenses = ____

Paycheque name: _____

Income		
Date	Details	Amount
Total		

Cash or virtual envelopes		
Date	Details	Amount
Total		

MONTH SIX

Bills and direct debits

Date	Details	Amount

Total

Debt pay-off

Date	Details	Amount

Total

CAZ MOONEY'S BUDGETING PLANNER

Sinking funds

Date	Details	Amount

Total

Savings

Date	Details	Amount

Total

Summary

	Amount
Income	
Bills and direct debits	
Cash or virtual envelopes	
Sinking funds	
Debt	
Savings	

Income minus expenses = ____

MONTH SIX

Paycheque name: _____

Income				Cash or virtual envelopes			
Date	Details		Amount	Date	Details		Amount
Total				Total			

CAZ MOONEY'S BUDGETING PLANNER

Bills and direct debits		
Date	Details	Amount
Total		

Debt pay-off		
Date	Details	Amount
Total		

MONTH SIX

Sinking funds

Date	Details	Amount

Total

Savings

Date	Details	Amount

Total

Summary

	Amount
Income	
Bills and direct debits	
Cash or virtual envelopes	
Sinking funds	
Debt	
Savings	

Income minus expenses = ____

Freezer inventory

At the start of every month, take a few minutes to complete a quick freezer inventory. This will help you to know exactly what you have at home, and you can use that information to create your meal plan, saving you time and money. See page 79 for an example of how this might look.

Protein		Vegetables	
	○○○○○○		○○○○○○
	○○○○○○		○○○○○○
	○○○○○○		○○○○○○
	○○○○○○		○○○○○○
	○○○○○○		○○○○○○

Meals		Snacks and treats	
	○○○○○○		○○○○○○
	○○○○○○		○○○○○○
	○○○○○○		○○○○○○
	○○○○○○		○○○○○○
	○○○○○○		○○○○○○

Miscellaneous			
	○○○○○○		○○○○○○
	○○○○○○		○○○○○○
	○○○○○○		○○○○○○
	○○○○○○		○○○○○○
	○○○○○○		○○○○○○

MONTH SIX

Meals I have at home

Making a note of meals that you already have at home will help reduce both food waste and the cost of your groceries. You may be short an ingredient or two for some meals, but the third column will make these easy to add to your shopping list. There's an example of this section on page 80.

Meal	Ingredients I already have	Ingredients I need

Monthly meal planner

Now it's time to plan your meals. This will help you to make efficient grocery lists and can be a great reminder to use up food that needs to be eaten. It's up to you whether you fill this section in weekly or monthly; there's an example of how I like to do it on page 82.

	Week one	Week two	Week three	Week four	Week five
Monday					
Tuesday					
Wednesday					
Thursday					
Friday					
Saturday					
Sunday					

MONTH SIX

Monthly spending tracker

Use this table to note where your money went this month. This will help you to reduce impulse spending and become more conscientious in how you spend your money. It's also very useful in helping you create your budget for the next month, as you can see where you need to allot your funds. See page 83 for a completed example of this tracker.

Date	Description	Category	Payment type	Amount

Monthly recap

It's time to look back over this month's finances. This section makes it easier to track your progress from month to month, and will help you to plan your financial goals for the next month. I've added an example of how I fill in this section on pages 84–6.

Income		
Category	Income type	Amount
	Total	

Spending		
Category	Spending type	Amount
	Total	

MONTH SIX

Extra debt payment

List debt					
Current total					
Minimum payment					
Extra payment					
Total paid					**Overall total paid**
New balance					

Savings and investments

List savings/ investments					
Paid in					
New balance					**Overall total paid**
Total paid					

Emergency fund balance: _____

Monthly wins

Use this calendar to record the things you've done right this month – whether that's cancelling a subscription that you no longer need, clearing a debt or starting an extra side hustle. I also like to use it to track my no-spend days – so any day that I don't spend anything on non-essentials, I'll colour in or sometimes mark with a little sticker star. Remember, every win, no matter how small, is bringing you one step closer to your goals!

Mon	Tue	Wed	Thu	Fri	Sat	Sun

Month: _____

> "Always celebrate the small wins"

CAZ MOONEY'S BUDGETING PLANNER

Your month at a glance

Use this calendar to record your paydays, along with the bills and direct debits that are due this month. I recommend using a highlighter to mark what needs to be paid from each paycheque in the same colour, and then you can record your totals in the key notes section. There's a full example of how I use this calendar on page 75.

Mon	Tue	Wed	Thu	Fri	Sat	Sun

Key notes
_____
_____
_____
_____

This month's goals

What goals are you hoping to achieve this month? Remember to set aims that will bring you closer to your six-month, one-year and five-year goals. To keep these goals achievable, make sure to write down the amount of money that you would like to save, pay off or earn. I have shared an example of how I lay out this section on page 76.

○ _____
○ _____
○ _____
○ _____
○ _____
○ _____

How am I going to achieve them?

Use this section to set out your plan to hit these goals. This will help you to keep them realistic.

○ _____
○ _____
○ _____
○ _____
○ _____
○ _____

Budget by paycheque

This is your plan for your paycheque. By now, you should feel confident filling this out, and there's a mock budget on pages 77–8 that will walk you through step by step. Once you've filled in your income, expenses and financial goals, your income minus expenses should equal zero, as you're giving every cent a job.

Paycheque name: _____

Income		
Date	Details	Amount
Total		

Cash or virtual envelopes		
Date	Details	Amount
Total		

MONTH SEVEN

Bills and direct debits		
Date	Details	Amount

Total

Debt pay-off		
Date	Details	Amount

Total

CAZ MOONEY'S BUDGETING PLANNER

Sinking funds

Date	Details	Amount
Total		

Savings

Date	Details	Amount
Total		

Summary

	Amount
Income	
Bills and direct debits	
Cash or virtual envelopes	
Sinking funds	
Debt	
Savings	

Income minus expenses = ____

MONTH SEVEN

Paycheque name: _____

Income		
Date	Details	Amount
Total		

Cash or virtual envelopes		
Date	Details	Amount
Total		

CAZ MOONEY'S BUDGETING PLANNER

Bills and direct debits		
Date	Details	Amount
Total		

Debt pay-off		
Date	Details	Amount
Total		

MONTH SEVEN

Sinking funds

Date	Details	Amount

Total

Savings

Date	Details	Amount

Total

Summary

	Amount
Income	
Bills and direct debits	
Cash or virtual envelopes	
Sinking funds	
Debt	
Savings	

Income minus expenses = ____

CAZ MOONEY'S BUDGETING PLANNER

Paycheque name: _____

Income				Cash or virtual envelopes			
Date	Details		Amount	Date	Details		Amount
Total				Total			

MONTH SEVEN

Bills and direct debits

Date	Details	Amount

Total

Debt pay-off

Date	Details	Amount

Total

CAZ MOONEY'S BUDGETING PLANNER

Sinking funds

Date	Details	Amount
Total		

Savings

Date	Details	Amount
Total		

Summary

	Amount
Income	
Bills and direct debits	
Cash or virtual envelopes	
Sinking funds	
Debt	
Savings	

Income minus expenses = ____

MONTH SEVEN

Paycheque name: _____

Income			
Date	Details		Amount
Total			

Cash or virtual envelopes			
Date	Details		Amount
Total			

CAZ MOONEY'S BUDGETING PLANNER

Bills and direct debits		
Date	Details	Amount
Total		

Debt pay-off		
Date	Details	Amount
Total		

MONTH SEVEN

Sinking funds

Date	Details	Amount

Total

Savings

Date	Details	Amount

Total

Summary

	Amount
Income	
Bills and direct debits	
Cash or virtual envelopes	
Sinking funds	
Debt	
Savings	

Income minus expenses = _____

CAZ MOONEY'S BUDGETING PLANNER

Paycheque name: _____

Income		
Date	Details	Amount
Total		

Cash or virtual envelopes		
Date	Details	Amount
Total		

MONTH SEVEN

Bills and direct debits		
Date	Details	Amount

Total

Debt pay-off		
Date	Details	Amount

Total

CAZ MOONEY'S BUDGETING PLANNER

Sinking funds

Date	Details	Amount
Total		

Savings

Date	Details	Amount
Total		

Summary

	Amount
Income	
Bills and direct debits	
Cash or virtual envelopes	
Sinking funds	
Debt	
Savings	

Income minus expenses = ____

MONTH SEVEN

Freezer inventory

At the start of every month, take a few minutes to complete a quick freezer inventory. This will help you to know exactly what you have at home, and you can use that information to create your meal plan, saving you time and money. See page 79 for an example of how this might look.

Protein		Vegetables	
	○○○○○○		○○○○○○
	○○○○○○		○○○○○○
	○○○○○○		○○○○○○
	○○○○○○		○○○○○○
	○○○○○○		○○○○○○

Meals		Snacks and treats	
	○○○○○○		○○○○○○
	○○○○○○		○○○○○○
	○○○○○○		○○○○○○
	○○○○○○		○○○○○○
	○○○○○○		○○○○○○

Miscellaneous			
	○○○○○○		○○○○○○
	○○○○○○		○○○○○○
	○○○○○○		○○○○○○
	○○○○○○		○○○○○○
	○○○○○○		○○○○○○

Meals I have at home

Making a note of meals that you already have at home will help reduce both food waste and the cost of your groceries. You may be short an ingredient or two for some meals, but the third column will make these easy to add to your shopping list. There's an example of this section on page 80.

Meal	Ingredients I already have	Ingredients I need

MONTH SEVEN

Monthly meal planner

Now it's time to plan your meals. This will help you to make efficient grocery lists and can be a great reminder to use up food that needs to be eaten. It's up to you whether you fill this section in weekly or monthly; there's an example of how I like to do it on page 82.

	Week one	Week two	Week three	Week four	Week five
Monday					
Tuesday					
Wednesday					
Thursday					
Friday					
Saturday					
Sunday					

CAZ MOONEY'S BUDGETING PLANNER

Monthly spending tracker

Use this table to note where your money went this month. This will help you to reduce impulse spending and become more conscientious in how you spend your money. It's also very useful in helping you create your budget for the next month, as you can see where you need to allot your funds. See page 83 for a completed example of this tracker.

Date	Description	Category	Payment type	Amount

Monthly recap

It's time to look back over this month's finances. This section makes it easier to track your progress from month to month, and will help you to plan your financial goals for the next month. I've added an example of how I fill in this section on pages 84–6.

Income

Category	Income type	Amount
		Total

Spending

Category	Spending type	Amount
		Total

CAZ MOONEY'S BUDGETING PLANNER

Extra debt payment

List debt					
Current total					
Minimum payment					
Extra payment					
Total paid					**Overall total paid**
New balance					

Savings and investments

List savings/investments					
Paid in					
New balance					**Overall total paid**
Total paid					

Emergency fund balance: _____

MONTH SEVEN

Monthly wins

Use this calendar to record the things you've done right this month – whether that's cancelling a subscription that you no longer need, clearing a debt or starting an extra side hustle. I also like to use it to track my no-spend days – so any day that I don't spend anything on non-essentials, I'll colour in or sometimes mark with a little sticker star. Remember, every win, no matter how small, is bringing you one step closer to your goals!

Mon	Tue	Wed	Thu	Fri	Sat	Sun

Month: _____

"Spending time with those you love is more important than spending money"

MONTH EIGHT

Your month at a glance

Use this calendar to record your paydays, along with the bills and direct debits that are due this month. I recommend using a highlighter to mark what needs to be paid from each paycheque in the same colour, and then you can record your totals in the key notes section. There's a full example of how I use this calendar on page 75.

Mon	Tue	Wed	Thu	Fri	Sat	Sun

Key notes
_____
_____
_____

This month's goals

What goals are you hoping to achieve this month? Remember to set aims that will bring you closer to your six-month, one-year and five-year goals. To keep these goals achievable, make sure to write down the amount of money that you would like to save, pay off or earn. I have shared an example of how I lay out this section on page 76.

○ _____

○ _____

○ _____

○ _____

○ _____

○ _____

How am I going to achieve them?

Use this section to set out your plan to hit these goals. This will help you to keep them realistic.

○ _____

○ _____

○ _____

○ _____

○ _____

○ _____

MONTH EIGHT

Budget by paycheque

This is your plan for your paycheque. By now, you should feel confident filling this out, and there's a mock budget on pages 77–8 that will walk you through step by step. Once you've filled in your income, expenses and financial goals, your income minus expenses should equal zero, as you're giving every cent a job.

Paycheque name: _____

Income			
Date	Details		Amount
Total			

Cash or virtual envelopes			
Date	Details		Amount
Total			

CAZ MOONEY'S BUDGETING PLANNER

Bills and direct debits		
Date	Details	Amount
Total		

Debt pay-off		
Date	Details	Amount
Total		

MONTH EIGHT

Sinking funds

Date	Details	Amount
Total		

Savings

Date	Details	Amount
Total		

Summary

	Amount
Income	
Bills and direct debits	
Cash or virtual envelopes	
Sinking funds	
Debt	
Savings	

Income minus expenses = ____

CAZ MOONEY'S BUDGETING PLANNER

Paycheque name: _____

Income		
Date	Details	Amount
Total		

Cash or virtual envelopes		
Date	Details	Amount
Total		

MONTH EIGHT

Bills and direct debits				Debt pay-off		
Date	Details	Amount		Date	Details	Amount
Total				Total		

CAZ MOONEY'S BUDGETING PLANNER

Sinking funds

Date	Details	Amount
Total		

Savings

Date	Details	Amount
Total		

Summary

	Amount
Income	
Bills and direct debits	
Cash or virtual envelopes	
Sinking funds	
Debt	
Savings	

Income minus expenses = ____

MONTH EIGHT

Paycheque name: _____

Income			
Date	Details		Amount
Total			

Cash or virtual envelopes			
Date	Details		Amount
Total			

CAZ MOONEY'S BUDGETING PLANNER

Bills and direct debits		
Date	Details	Amount
Total		

Debt pay-off		
Date	Details	Amount
Total		

MONTH EIGHT

Sinking funds

Date	Details	Amount

Total

Savings

Date	Details	Amount

Total

Summary

	Amount
Income	
Bills and direct debits	
Cash or virtual envelopes	
Sinking funds	
Debt	
Savings	

Income minus expenses = ____

CAZ MOONEY'S BUDGETING PLANNER

Paycheque name: _____

Income		
Date	Details	Amount
Total		

Cash or virtual envelopes		
Date	Details	Amount
Total		

MONTH EIGHT

Bills and direct debits			Debt pay-off		
Date	Details	Amount	Date	Details	Amount
Total			Total		

CAZ MOONEY'S BUDGETING PLANNER

Sinking funds

Date	Details	Amount
Total		

Savings

Date	Details	Amount
Total		

Summary

	Amount
Income	
Bills and direct debits	
Cash or virtual envelopes	
Sinking funds	
Debt	
Savings	

Income minus expenses = _____

MONTH EIGHT

Paycheque name: _____

Income				Cash or virtual envelopes			
Date	Details		Amount	Date	Details		Amount
Total				Total			

CAZ MOONEY'S BUDGETING PLANNER

Bills and direct debits		
Date	Details	Amount
Total		

Debt pay-off		
Date	Details	Amount
Total		

MONTH EIGHT

Sinking funds

Date	Details	Amount
Total		

Savings

Date	Details	Amount
Total		

Summary

	Amount
Income	
Bills and direct debits	
Cash or virtual envelopes	
Sinking funds	
Debt	
Savings	

Income minus expenses = ____

Freezer inventory

At the start of every month, take a few minutes to complete a quick freezer inventory. This will help you to know exactly what you have at home, and you can use that information to create your meal plan, saving you time and money. See page 79 for an example of how this might look.

Protein		Vegetables	
	○○○○○○		○○○○○○
	○○○○○○		○○○○○○
	○○○○○○		○○○○○○
	○○○○○○		○○○○○○
	○○○○○○		○○○○○○

Meals		Snacks and treats	
	○○○○○○		○○○○○○
	○○○○○○		○○○○○○
	○○○○○○		○○○○○○
	○○○○○○		○○○○○○
	○○○○○○		○○○○○○

Miscellaneous			
	○○○○○○		○○○○○○
	○○○○○○		○○○○○○
	○○○○○○		○○○○○○
	○○○○○○		○○○○○○
	○○○○○○		○○○○○○

MONTH EIGHT

Meals I have at home

Making a note of meals that you already have at home will help reduce both food waste and the cost of your groceries. You may be short an ingredient or two for some meals, but the third column will make these easy to add to your shopping list. There's an example of this section on page 80.

Meal	Ingredients I already have	Ingredients I need

Monthly meal planner

Now it's time to plan your meals. This will help you to make efficient grocery lists and can be a great reminder to use up food that needs to be eaten. It's up to you whether you fill this section in weekly or monthly; there's an example of how I like to do it on page 82.

	Week one	Week two	Week three	Week four	Week five
Monday					
Tuesday					
Wednesday					
Thursday					
Friday					
Saturday					
Sunday					

MONTH EIGHT

Monthly spending tracker

Use this table to note where your money went this month. This will help you to reduce impulse spending and become more conscientious in how you spend your money. It's also very useful in helping you create your budget for the next month, as you can see where you need to allot your funds. See page 83 for a completed example of this tracker.

Date	Description	Category	Payment type	Amount

Monthly recap

It's time to look back over this month's finances. This section makes it easier to track your progress from month to month, and will help you to plan your financial goals for the next month. I've added an example of how I fill in this section on pages 84–6.

Income		
Category	Income type	Amount
	Total	

Spending		
Category	Spending type	Amount
	Total	

MONTH EIGHT

Extra debt payment

List debt					
Current total					
Minimum payment					
Extra payment					
Total paid					**Overall total paid**
New balance					

Savings and investments

List savings/investments					
Paid in					
New balance					**Overall total paid**
Total paid					

Emergency fund balance: _____

Monthly wins

Use this calendar to record the things you've done right this month — whether that's cancelling a subscription that you no longer need, clearing a debt or starting an extra side hustle. I also like to use it to track my no-spend days — so any day that I don't spend anything on non-essentials, I'll colour in or sometimes mark with a little sticker star. Remember, every win, no matter how small, is bringing you one step closer to your goals!

Mon	Tue	Wed	Thu	Fri	Sat	Sun

Month: _____

> "Make your 'why' louder than your excuses"

CAZ MOONEY'S BUDGETING PLANNER

Your month at a glance

Use this calendar to record your paydays, along with the bills and direct debits that are due this month. I recommend using a highlighter to mark what needs to be paid from each paycheque in the same colour, and then you can record your totals in the key notes section. There's a full example of how I use this calendar on page 75.

Mon	Tue	Wed	Thu	Fri	Sat	Sun

Key notes

_____
_____
_____
_____

This month's goals

What goals are you hoping to achieve this month? Remember to set aims that will bring you closer to your six-month, one-year and five-year goals. To keep these goals achievable, make sure to write down the amount of money that you would like to save, pay off or earn. I have shared an example of how I lay out this section on page 76.

- _____
- _____
- _____
- _____
- _____
- _____

How am I going to achieve them?

Use this section to set out your plan to hit these goals. This will help you to keep them realistic.

- _____
- _____
- _____
- _____
- _____
- _____

Budget by paycheque

This is your plan for your paycheque. By now, you should feel confident filling this out, and there's a mock budget on pages 77–8 that will walk you through step by step. Once you've filled in your income, expenses and financial goals, your income minus expenses should equal zero, as you're giving every cent a job.

Paycheque name: _____

Income		
Date	Details	Amount
Total		

Cash or virtual envelopes		
Date	Details	Amount
Total		

MONTH NINE

Bills and direct debits				Debt pay-off			
Date	Details		Amount	Date	Details		Amount

Total / Total

CAZ MOONEY'S BUDGETING PLANNER

Sinking funds

Date	Details	Amount
Total		

Savings

Date	Details	Amount
Total		

Summary

	Amount
Income	
Bills and direct debits	
Cash or virtual envelopes	
Sinking funds	
Debt	
Savings	

Income minus expenses = ____

MONTH NINE

Paycheque name: _____

Income			
Date	Details		Amount

Total

Cash or virtual envelopes			
Date	Details		Amount

Total

CAZ MOONEY'S BUDGETING PLANNER

Bills and direct debits

Date	Details	Amount
Total		

Debt pay-off

Date	Details	Amount
Total		

MONTH NINE

Sinking funds

Date	Details	Amount

Total

Savings

Date	Details	Amount

Total

Summary

	Amount
Income	
Bills and direct debits	
Cash or virtual envelopes	
Sinking funds	
Debt	
Savings	

Income minus expenses = ____

CAZ MOONEY'S BUDGETING PLANNER

Paycheque name: _____

Income		
Date	Details	Amount
Total		

Cash or virtual envelopes		
Date	Details	Amount
Total		

MONTH NINE

Bills and direct debits		
Date	Details	Amount
Total		

Debt pay-off		
Date	Details	Amount
Total		

CAZ MOONEY'S BUDGETING PLANNER

Sinking funds

Date	Details	Amount
Total		

Savings

Date	Details	Amount
Total		

Summary

	Amount
Income	
Bills and direct debits	
Cash or virtual envelopes	
Sinking funds	
Debt	
Savings	

Income minus expenses = ____

MONTH NINE

Paycheque name: _____

Income				Cash or virtual envelopes		
Date	Details		Amount	Date	Details	Amount
Total				Total		

CAZ MOONEY'S BUDGETING PLANNER

Bills and direct debits		
Date	Details	Amount
Total		

Debt pay-off		
Date	Details	Amount
Total		

Sinking funds

Date	Details	Amount
Total		

Savings

Date	Details	Amount
Total		

Summary

	Amount
Income	
Bills and direct debits	
Cash or virtual envelopes	
Sinking funds	
Debt	
Savings	

Income minus expenses = ____

Paycheque name: _____

Income				Cash or virtual envelopes		
Date	Details	Amount		Date	Details	Amount
Total				Total		

MONTH NINE

Bills and direct debits

Date	Details	Amount

Total

Debt pay-off

Date	Details	Amount

Total

Sinking funds

Date	Details	Amount

Total

Savings

Date	Details	Amount

Total

Summary

	Amount
Income	
Bills and direct debits	
Cash or virtual envelopes	
Sinking funds	
Debt	
Savings	

Income minus expenses = ____

MONTH NINE

Freezer inventory

At the start of every month, take a few minutes to complete a quick freezer inventory. This will help you to know exactly what you have at home, and you can use that information to create your meal plan, saving you time and money. See page 79 for an example of how this might look.

Protein		Vegetables	
	○○○○○○		○○○○○○
	○○○○○○		○○○○○○
	○○○○○○		○○○○○○
	○○○○○○		○○○○○○
	○○○○○○		○○○○○○

Meals		Snacks and treats	
	○○○○○○		○○○○○○
	○○○○○○		○○○○○○
	○○○○○○		○○○○○○
	○○○○○○		○○○○○○
	○○○○○○		○○○○○○

Miscellaneous			
	○○○○○○		○○○○○○
	○○○○○○		○○○○○○
	○○○○○○		○○○○○○
	○○○○○○		○○○○○○
	○○○○○○		○○○○○○

Meals I have at home

Making a note of meals that you already have at home will help reduce both food waste and the cost of your groceries. You may be short an ingredient or two for some meals, but the third column will make these easy to add to your shopping list. There's an example of this section on page 80.

Meal	Ingredients I already have	Ingredients I need

MONTH NINE

Monthly meal planner

Now it's time to plan your meals. This will help you to make efficient grocery lists and can be a great reminder to use up food that needs to be eaten. It's up to you whether you fill this section in weekly or monthly; there's an example of how I like to do it on page 82.

	Week one	Week two	Week three	Week four	Week five
Monday					
Tuesday					
Wednesday					
Thursday					
Friday					
Saturday					
Sunday					

Monthly spending tracker

Use this table to note where your money went this month. This will help you to reduce impulse spending and become more conscientious in how you spend your money. It's also very useful in helping you create your budget for the next month, as you can see where you need to allot your funds. See page 83 for a completed example of this tracker.

Date	Description	Category	Payment type	Amount

Monthly recap

It's time to look back over this month's finances. This section makes it easier to track your progress from month to month, and will help you to plan your financial goals for the next month. I've added an example of how I fill in this section on pages 84–6.

Income		
Category	Income type	Amount
	Total	

Spending		
Category	Spending type	Amount
	Total	

Extra debt payment

List debt					
Current total					
Minimum payment					
Extra payment					
Total paid					**Overall total paid**
New balance					

Savings and investments

List savings/investments					
Paid in					
New balance					**Overall total paid**
Total paid					

Emergency fund balance: _____

MONTH NINE

Monthly wins

Use this calendar to record the things you've done right this month – whether that's cancelling a subscription that you no longer need, clearing a debt or starting an extra side hustle. I also like to use it to track my no-spend days – so any day that I don't spend anything on non-essentials, I'll colour in or sometimes mark with a little sticker star. Remember, every win, no matter how small, is bringing you one step closer to your goals!

Mon	Tue	Wed	Thu	Fri	Sat	Sun

Month: _____

> **" Reach those goals and turn the invisible visible "**

MONTH TEN

Your month at a glance

Use this calendar to record your paydays, along with the bills and direct debits that are due this month. I recommend using a highlighter to mark what needs to be paid from each paycheque in the same colour, and then you can record your totals in the key notes section. There's a full example of how I use this calendar on page 75.

Mon	Tue	Wed	Thu	Fri	Sat	Sun

Key notes
_____
_____
_____

This month's goals

What goals are you hoping to achieve this month? Remember to set aims that will bring you closer to your six-month, one-year and five-year goals. To keep these goals achievable, make sure to write down the amount of money that you would like to save, pay off or earn. I have shared an example of how I lay out this section on page 76.

- _____
- _____
- _____
- _____
- _____
- _____

How am I going to achieve them?

Use this section to set out your plan to hit these goals. This will help you to keep them realistic.

- _____
- _____
- _____
- _____
- _____
- _____

MONTH TEN

Budget by paycheque

This is your plan for your paycheque. By now, you should feel confident filling this out, and there's a mock budget on pages 77–8 that will walk you through step by step. Once you've filled in your income, expenses and financial goals, your income minus expenses should equal zero, as you're giving every cent a job.

Paycheque name: _____

Income		
Date	Details	Amount
Total		

Cash or virtual envelopes		
Date	Details	Amount
Total		

CAZ MOONEY'S BUDGETING PLANNER

Bills and direct debits		
Date	Details	Amount
Total		

Debt pay-off		
Date	Details	Amount
Total		

MONTH TEN

Sinking funds

Date	Details	Amount

Total

Savings

Date	Details	Amount

Total

Summary

	Amount
Income	
Bills and direct debits	
Cash or virtual envelopes	
Sinking funds	
Debt	
Savings	

Income minus expenses = ____

CAZ MOONEY'S BUDGETING PLANNER

Paycheque name: _____

Income		
Date	Details	Amount

Total

Cash or virtual envelopes		
Date	Details	Amount

Total

MONTH TEN

Bills and direct debits		
Date	Details	Amount
Total		

Debt pay-off		
Date	Details	Amount
Total		

CAZ MOONEY'S BUDGETING PLANNER

Sinking funds

Date	Details	Amount
Total		

Savings

Date	Details	Amount
Total		

Summary

	Amount
Income	
Bills and direct debits	
Cash or virtual envelopes	
Sinking funds	
Debt	
Savings	

Income minus expenses = ____

MONTH TEN

Paycheque name: _____

Income				Cash or virtual envelopes			
Date	Details		Amount	Date	Details		Amount
Total				Total			

CAZ MOONEY'S BUDGETING PLANNER

Bills and direct debits

Date	Details	Amount
Total		

Debt pay-off

Date	Details	Amount
Total		

MONTH TEN

Sinking funds

Date	Details	Amount

Total

Savings

Date	Details	Amount

Total

Summary

	Amount
Income	
Bills and direct debits	
Cash or virtual envelopes	
Sinking funds	
Debt	
Savings	

Income minus expenses = _____

CAZ MOONEY'S BUDGETING PLANNER

Paycheque name: _____

Income		
Date	Details	Amount
Total		

Cash or virtual envelopes		
Date	Details	Amount
Total		

MONTH TEN

Bills and direct debits

Date	Details	Amount

Total

Debt pay-off

Date	Details	Amount

Total

CAZ MOONEY'S BUDGETING PLANNER

Sinking funds

Date	Details	Amount
Total		

Savings

Date	Details	Amount
Total		

Summary

	Amount
Income	
Bills and direct debits	
Cash or virtual envelopes	
Sinking funds	
Debt	
Savings	

Income minus expenses = _____

MONTH TEN

Paycheque name: _____

Income				Cash or virtual envelopes			
Date	Details		Amount	Date	Details		Amount
Total				Total			

CAZ MOONEY'S BUDGETING PLANNER

Bills and direct debits

Date	Details	Amount
Total		

Debt pay-off

Date	Details	Amount
Total		

MONTH TEN

Sinking funds

Date	Details	Amount

Total

Savings

Date	Details	Amount

Total

Summary

	Amount
Income	
Bills and direct debits	
Cash or virtual envelopes	
Sinking funds	
Debt	
Savings	

Income minus expenses = ____

Freezer inventory

At the start of every month, take a few minutes to complete a quick freezer inventory. This will help you to know exactly what you have at home, and you can use that information to create your meal plan, saving you time and money. See page 79 for an example of how this might look.

Protein		Vegetables	
	○○○○○○		○○○○○○
	○○○○○○		○○○○○○
	○○○○○○		○○○○○○
	○○○○○○		○○○○○○
	○○○○○○		○○○○○○
Meals		**Snacks and treats**	
	○○○○○○		○○○○○○
	○○○○○○		○○○○○○
	○○○○○○		○○○○○○
	○○○○○○		○○○○○○
	○○○○○○		○○○○○○
Miscellaneous			
	○○○○○○		○○○○○○
	○○○○○○		○○○○○○
	○○○○○○		○○○○○○
	○○○○○○		○○○○○○
	○○○○○○		○○○○○○

Meals I have at home

Making a note of meals that you already have at home will help reduce both food waste and the cost of your groceries. You may be short an ingredient or two for some meals, but the third column will make these easy to add to your shopping list. There's an example of this section on page 80.

Meal	Ingredients I already have	Ingredients I need

Monthly meal planner

Now it's time to plan your meals. This will help you to make efficient grocery lists and can be a great reminder to use up food that needs to be eaten. It's up to you whether you fill this section in weekly or monthly; there's an example of how I like to do it on page 82.

	Week one	Week two	Week three	Week four	Week five
Monday					
Tuesday					
Wednesday					
Thursday					
Friday					
Saturday					
Sunday					

MONTH TEN

Monthly spending tracker

Use this table to note where your money went this month. This will help you to reduce impulse spending and become more conscientious in how you spend your money. It's also very useful in helping you create your budget for the next month, as you can see where you need to allot your funds. See page 83 for a completed example of this tracker.

Date	Description	Category	Payment type	Amount

Monthly recap

It's time to look back over this month's finances. This section makes it easier to track your progress from month to month, and will help you to plan your financial goals for the next month. I've added an example of how I fill in this section on pages 84–6.

Income		
Category	Income type	Amount
	Total	

Spending		
Category	Spending type	Amount
	Total	

MONTH TEN

Extra debt payment

List debt					
Current total					
Minimum payment					
Extra payment					
Total paid					**Overall total paid**
New balance					

Savings and investments

List savings/ investments					
Paid in					
New balance					**Overall total paid**
Total paid					

Emergency fund balance: _____

Monthly wins

Use this calendar to record the things you've done right this month – whether that's cancelling a subscription that you no longer need, clearing a debt or starting an extra side hustle. I also like to use it to track my no-spend days – so any day that I don't spend anything on non-essentials, I'll colour in or sometimes mark with a little sticker star. Remember, every win, no matter how small, is bringing you one step closer to your goals!

Mon	Tue	Wed	Thu	Fri	Sat	Sun

Month: _____

" Budgeting is for everyone who wants a better financial future "

Your month at a glance

Use this calendar to record your paydays, along with the bills and direct debits that are due this month. I recommend using a highlighter to mark what needs to be paid from each paycheque in the same colour, and then you can record your totals in the key notes section. There's a full example of how I use this calendar on page 75.

Mon	Tue	Wed	Thu	Fri	Sat	Sun

Key notes

_____
_____
_____
_____

MONTH ELEVEN

This month's goals

What goals are you hoping to achieve this month? Remember to set aims that will bring you closer to your six-month, one-year and five-year goals. To keep these goals achievable, make sure to write down the amount of money that you would like to save, pay off or earn. I have shared an example of how I lay out this section on page 76.

○ _____
○ _____
○ _____
○ _____
○ _____
○ _____

How am I going to achieve them?

Use this section to set out your plan to hit these goals. This will help you to keep them realistic.

○ _____
○ _____
○ _____
○ _____
○ _____
○ _____

Budget by paycheque

This is your plan for your paycheque. By now, you should feel confident filling this out, and there's a mock budget on pages 77–8 that will walk you through step by step. Once you've filled in your income, expenses and financial goals, your income minus expenses should equal zero, as you're giving every cent a job.

Paycheque name: _____

Income		
Date	Details	Amount
Total		

Cash or virtual envelopes		
Date	Details	Amount
Total		

MONTH ELEVEN

Bills and direct debits		
Date	Details	Amount

Total

Debt pay-off		
Date	Details	Amount

Total

CAZ MOONEY'S BUDGETING PLANNER

Sinking funds

Date	Details	Amount
Total		

Savings

Date	Details	Amount
Total		

Summary

	Amount
Income	
Bills and direct debits	
Cash or virtual envelopes	
Sinking funds	
Debt	
Savings	

Income minus expenses = ____

Paycheque name: _____

Income		
Date	Details	Amount
Total		

Cash or virtual envelopes		
Date	Details	Amount
Total		

CAZ MOONEY'S BUDGETING PLANNER

Bills and direct debits

Date	Details	Amount
Total		

Debt pay-off

Date	Details	Amount
Total		

Sinking funds

Date	Details	Amount
Total		

Savings

Date	Details	Amount
Total		

Summary

	Amount
Income	
Bills and direct debits	
Cash or virtual envelopes	
Sinking funds	
Debt	
Savings	

Income minus expenses = _____

CAZ MOONEY'S BUDGETING PLANNER

Paycheque name: _____

Income				Cash or virtual envelopes		
Date	Details		Amount	Date	Details	Amount
Total				Total		

MONTH ELEVEN

Bills and direct debits		
Date	Details	Amount
Total		

Debt pay-off		
Date	Details	Amount
Total		

CAZ MOONEY'S BUDGETING PLANNER

Sinking funds

Date	Details	Amount
Total		

Savings

Date	Details	Amount
Total		

Summary

	Amount
Income	
Bills and direct debits	
Cash or virtual envelopes	
Sinking funds	
Debt	
Savings	

Income minus expenses = ____

MONTH ELEVEN

Paycheque name: _____

Income		
Date	Details	Amount
Total		

Cash or virtual envelopes		
Date	Details	Amount
Total		

CAZ MOONEY'S BUDGETING PLANNER

Bills and direct debits

Date	Details	Amount
Total		

Debt pay-off

Date	Details	Amount
Total		

MONTH ELEVEN

Sinking funds

Date	Details	Amount
Total		

Savings

Date	Details	Amount
Total		

Summary

	Amount
Income	
Bills and direct debits	
Cash or virtual envelopes	
Sinking funds	
Debt	
Savings	

Income minus expenses = ____

Paycheque name: _____

Income		
Date	Details	Amount
Total		

Cash or virtual envelopes		
Date	Details	Amount
Total		

MONTH ELEVEN

Bills and direct debits		
Date	Details	Amount
Total		

Debt pay-off		
Date	Details	Amount
Total		

CAZ MOONEY'S BUDGETING PLANNER

Sinking funds

Date	Details	Amount

Total

Savings

Date	Details	Amount

Total

Summary

	Amount
Income	
Bills and direct debits	
Cash or virtual envelopes	
Sinking funds	
Debt	
Savings	

Income minus expenses = ____

MONTH ELEVEN

Freezer inventory

At the start of every month, take a few minutes to complete a quick freezer inventory. This will help you to know exactly what you have at home, and you can use that information to create your meal plan, saving you time and money. See page 79 for an example of how this might look.

Protein		Vegetables	
	○○○○○○		○○○○○○
	○○○○○○		○○○○○○
	○○○○○○		○○○○○○
	○○○○○○		○○○○○○
	○○○○○○		○○○○○○

Meals		Snacks and treats	
	○○○○○○		○○○○○○
	○○○○○○		○○○○○○
	○○○○○○		○○○○○○
	○○○○○○		○○○○○○
	○○○○○○		○○○○○○

Miscellaneous			
	○○○○○○		○○○○○○
	○○○○○○		○○○○○○
	○○○○○○		○○○○○○
	○○○○○○		○○○○○○
	○○○○○○		○○○○○○

Meals I have at home

Making a note of meals that you already have at home will help reduce both food waste and the cost of your groceries. You may be short an ingredient or two for some meals, but the third column will make these easy to add to your shopping list. There's an example of this section on page 80.

Meal	Ingredients I already have	Ingredients I need

MONTH ELEVEN

Monthly meal planner

Now it's time to plan your meals. This will help you to make efficient grocery lists and can be a great reminder to use up food that needs to be eaten. It's up to you whether you fill this section in weekly or monthly; there's an example of how I like to do it on page 82.

	Week one	Week two	Week three	Week four	Week five
Monday					
Tuesday					
Wednesday					
Thursday					
Friday					
Saturday					
Sunday					

Monthly spending tracker

Use this table to note where your money went this month. This will help you to reduce impulse spending and become more conscientious in how you spend your money. It's also very useful in helping you create your budget for the next month, as you can see where you need to allot your funds. See page 83 for a completed example of this tracker.

Date	Description	Category	Payment type	Amount

Monthly recap

It's time to look back over this month's finances. This section makes it easier to track your progress from month to month, and will help you to plan your financial goals for the next month. I've added an example of how I fill in this section on pages 84–6.

Income

Category	Income type	Amount
	Total	

Spending

Category	Spending type	Amount
	Total	

CAZ MOONEY'S BUDGETING PLANNER

Extra debt payment

List debt					
Current total					
Minimum payment					
Extra payment					
Total paid					**Overall total paid**
New balance					

Savings and investments

List savings/investments					
Paid in					
New balance					**Overall total paid**
Total paid					

Emergency fund balance: _____

MONTH ELEVEN

Monthly wins

Use this calendar to record the things you've done right this month – whether that's cancelling a subscription that you no longer need, clearing a debt or starting an extra side hustle. I also like to use it to track my no-spend days – so any day that I don't spend anything on non-essentials, I'll colour in or sometimes mark with a little sticker star. Remember, every win, no matter how small, is bringing you one step closer to your goals!

Mon	Tue	Wed	Thu	Fri	Sat	Sun

Month: _____

> "It's time to prioritise what matters most to you"

MONTH TWELVE

Your month at a glance

Use this calendar to record your paydays, along with the bills and direct debits that are due this month. I recommend using a highlighter to mark what needs to be paid from each paycheque in the same colour, and then you can record your totals in the key notes section. There's a full example of how I use this calendar on page 75.

Mon	Tue	Wed	Thu	Fri	Sat	Sun

Key notes

_____

_____

_____

This month's goals

What goals are you hoping to achieve this month? Remember to set aims that will bring you closer to your six-month, one-year and five-year goals. To keep these goals achievable, make sure to write down the amount of money that you would like to save, pay off or earn. I have shared an example of how I lay out this section on page 76.

- _____
- _____
- _____
- _____
- _____
- _____

How am I going to achieve them?

Use this section to set out your plan to hit these goals. This will help you to keep them realistic.

- _____
- _____
- _____
- _____
- _____
- _____

MONTH TWELVE

Budget by paycheque

This is your plan for your paycheque. By now, you should feel confident filling this out, and there's a mock budget on pages 77–8 that will walk you through step by step. Once you've filled in your income, expenses and financial goals, your income minus expenses should equal zero, as you're giving every cent a job.

Paycheque name: _____

Income		
Date	Details	Amount
Total		

Cash or virtual envelopes		
Date	Details	Amount
Total		

CAZ MOONEY'S BUDGETING PLANNER

Bills and direct debits		
Date	Details	Amount
Total		

Debt pay-off		
Date	Details	Amount
Total		

MONTH TWELVE

Sinking funds

Date	Details	Amount

Total

Savings

Date	Details	Amount

Total

Summary

	Amount
Income	
Bills and direct debits	
Cash or virtual envelopes	
Sinking funds	
Debt	
Savings	

Income minus expenses = _____

CAZ MOONEY'S BUDGETING PLANNER

Paycheque name: _____

Income		
Date	Details	Amount
Total		

Cash or virtual envelopes		
Date	Details	Amount
Total		

MONTH TWELVE

Bills and direct debits		
Date	Details	Amount
Total		

Debt pay-off		
Date	Details	Amount
Total		

CAZ MOONEY'S BUDGETING PLANNER

Sinking funds

Date	Details	Amount
Total		

Savings

Date	Details	Amount
Total		

Summary

	Amount
Income	
Bills and direct debits	
Cash or virtual envelopes	
Sinking funds	
Debt	
Savings	

Income minus expenses = ____

Paycheque name: _____

Income		
Date	Details	Amount
Total		

Cash or virtual envelopes		
Date	Details	Amount
Total		

CAZ MOONEY'S BUDGETING PLANNER

Bills and direct debits		
Date	Details	Amount
Total		

Debt pay-off		
Date	Details	Amount
Total		

MONTH TWELVE

Sinking funds

Date	Details	Amount

Total

Savings

Date	Details	Amount

Total

Summary

	Amount
Income	
Bills and direct debits	
Cash or virtual envelopes	
Sinking funds	
Debt	
Savings	

Income minus expenses = ____

CAZ MOONEY'S BUDGETING PLANNER

Paycheque name: _____

Income				Cash or virtual envelopes			
Date	Details		Amount	Date	Details		Amount
Total				Total			

MONTH TWELVE

Bills and direct debits		
Date	Details	Amount
Total		

Debt pay-off		
Date	Details	Amount
Total		

CAZ MOONEY'S BUDGETING PLANNER

Sinking funds

Date	Details	Amount
Total		

Savings

Date	Details	Amount
Total		

Summary

	Amount
Income	
Bills and direct debits	
Cash or virtual envelopes	
Sinking funds	
Debt	
Savings	

Income minus expenses = ____

MONTH TWELVE

Paycheque name: _____

Income			
Date	Details		Amount
Total			

Cash or virtual envelopes			
Date	Details		Amount
Total			

CAZ MOONEY'S BUDGETING PLANNER

Bills and direct debits		
Date	Details	Amount
Total		

Debt pay-off		
Date	Details	Amount
Total		

MONTH TWELVE

Sinking funds

Date	Details	Amount
Total		

Savings

Date	Details	Amount
Total		

Summary

	Amount
Income	
Bills and direct debits	
Cash or virtual envelopes	
Sinking funds	
Debt	
Savings	

Income minus expenses = ____

Freezer inventory

At the start of every month, take a few minutes to complete a quick freezer inventory. This will help you to know exactly what you have at home, and you can use that information to create your meal plan, saving you time and money. See page 79 for an example of how this might look.

Protein	Vegetables
○○○○○○	○○○○○○
○○○○○○	○○○○○○
○○○○○○	○○○○○○
○○○○○○	○○○○○○
○○○○○○	○○○○○○

Meals	Snacks and treats
○○○○○○	○○○○○○
○○○○○○	○○○○○○
○○○○○○	○○○○○○
○○○○○○	○○○○○○
○○○○○○	○○○○○○

Miscellaneous	
○○○○○○	○○○○○○
○○○○○○	○○○○○○
○○○○○○	○○○○○○
○○○○○○	○○○○○○
○○○○○○	○○○○○○

MONTH TWELVE

Meals I have at home

Making a note of meals that you already have at home will help reduce both food waste and the cost of your groceries. You may be short an ingredient or two for some meals, but the third column will make these easy to add to your shopping list. There's an example of this section on page 80.

Meal	Ingredients I already have	Ingredients I need

Monthly meal planner

Now it's time to plan your meals. This will help you to make efficient grocery lists and can be a great reminder to use up food that needs to be eaten. It's up to you whether you fill this section in weekly or monthly; there's an example of how I like to do it on page 82.

	Week one	Week two	Week three	Week four	Week five
Monday					
Tuesday					
Wednesday					
Thursday					
Friday					
Saturday					
Sunday					

Monthly spending tracker

Use this table to note where your money went this month. This will help you to reduce impulse spending and become more conscientious in how you spend your money. It's also very useful in helping you create your budget for the next month, as you can see where you need to allot your funds. See page 83 for a completed example of this tracker.

Date	Description	Category	Payment type	Amount

CAZ MOONEY'S BUDGETING PLANNER

Monthly recap

It's time to look back over this month's finances. This section makes it easier to track your progress from month to month, and will help you to plan your financial goals for the next month. I've added an example of how I fill in this section on pages 84–6.

Income

Category	Income type	Amount
	Total	

Spending

Category	Spending type	Amount
	Total	

MONTH TWELVE

Extra debt payment

List debt					
Current total					
Minimum payment					
Extra payment					
Total paid					**Overall total paid**
New balance					

Savings and investments

List savings/ investments					
Paid in					
New balance					**Overall total paid**
Total paid					

Emergency fund balance: _____

Monthly wins

Use this calendar to record the things you've done right this month — whether that's cancelling a subscription that you no longer need, clearing a debt or starting an extra side hustle. I also like to use it to track my no-spend days — so any day that I don't spend anything on non-essentials, I'll colour in or sometimes mark with a little sticker star. Remember, every win, no matter how small, is bringing you one step closer to your goals!

Mon	Tue	Wed	Thu	Fri	Sat	Sun

MONTH TWELVE

In case of emergency

While it's so important to keep your figures up to date in the monthly sections, I also love to track my savings in a more visual way. As we've discussed, €1,000 is a solid goal for your emergency fund, so I've added a tracker below that will chart your journey to this total. Each hexagon represents €20; colour one in or tick one off for every €20 that you save into this fund. Once you've filled them all in, you'll have saved your full emergency fund.

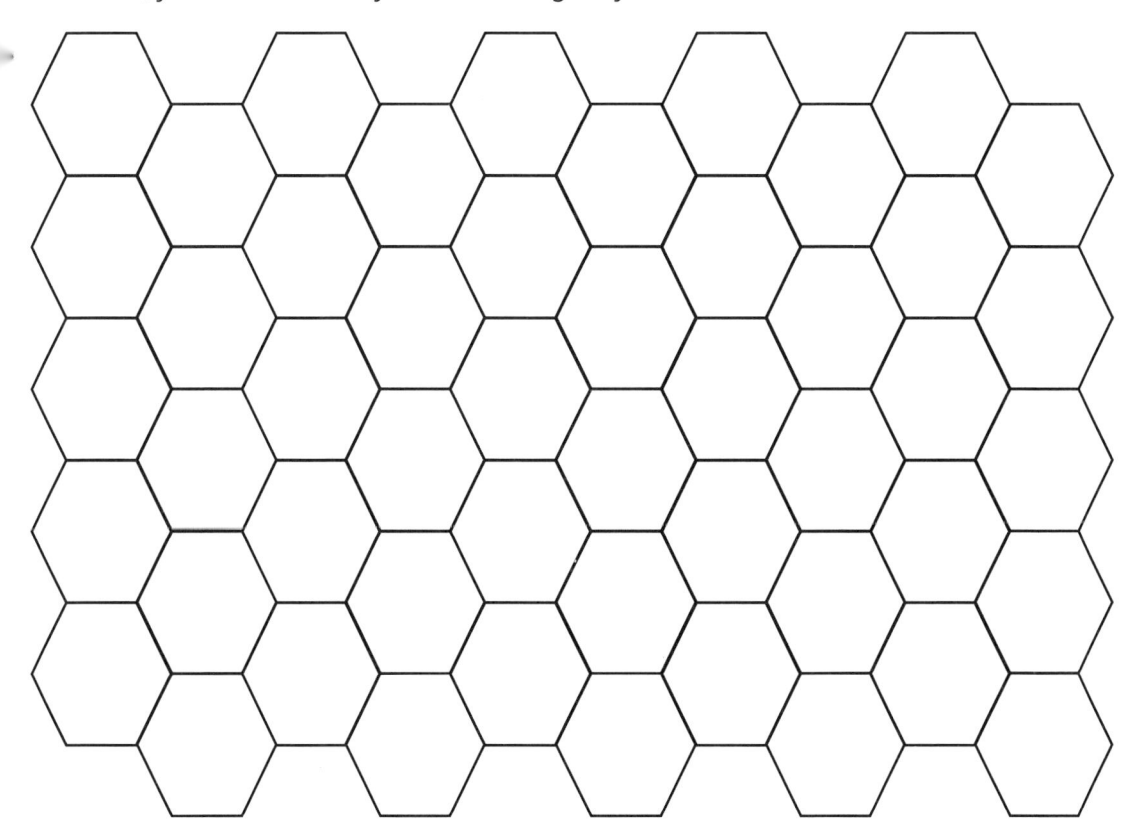

You can try doing this for other sinking funds and financial goals, too. Just divide the total amount that you need to save by the number of sections you want to include in a pattern or drawing. Then each section represents that smaller amount – and each time you add that amount to your fund, you'll get to colour in or tick off a section.

Acknowledgements

I would like to take a moment to thank my family — my wonderful husband and three amazing kids. Thank you for allowing me to share our financial journey so openly. Thank you for your patience, encouragement and all of your help over the last few months. Without you, none of this would be possible.

Thanks to my mum, my dad and my mother-in-law; you have been amazing and I am so blessed! Thank you for all your support, your advice and for helping me to become who I am today.

Thank you to my siblings, my biggest stans. The slagging has been surprisingly minimal!

Thank you to my friends, both here and abroad, and to those that I have met since I started sharing my journey. You guys know who you are. I am so lucky to have you.

Thank you to my agent, Tara Moriarty, for believing in me and understanding my mission. What a journey!

Lastly, and most importantly, I want to thank all of you. Thank you for your support throughout the last year. I cannot express the joy it brings when you share your own financial journeys and then your wins with me. I feel so lucky to be a part, however small, in your financial journeys. For me, honestly, that is what it is all about.